HOOK
TO
BOOKED

The 4-Stage System That Turns Strangers
into Qualified, Ready-to-Buy Clients

GABRIEL RYAN

GrowthMap Publishing

Hook to Booked

The 4-Stage System That Turns Strangers into
Qualified, Ready-to-Buy Clients

ISBN 979-8-9930766-0-7 Paperback

Diagrams designed by the author, Gabriel Ryan

Publisher: GrowthMap Holdings LLC

Printed in the United States of America

To Carlie, you've held my attention from the start.

CONTENTS

INTRODUCTION

Why 99% of Service Businesses Are One System Away From Never Worrying About Leads Again

---

I stared at my phone in disbelief.

"I can't believe we cleared $700,000," Cole texted me.

"Called it," I replied.

"You did. Final number = $772,350. Let's go!" he shot back.

I put the phone down and looked up at the ceiling of my home office.

It worked.

It totally freaking worked.

The system we'd built together, **deploying a simple marketing framework**, had just generated more revenue in seven days than Cole's previous best campaign by nearly 400%.

But here's the thing that really got me...

We didn't run fancy ads.

We didn't hire expensive agencies.

We didn't even build complicated funnels.

We simply focused on the things keeping his people up at night.

We dug into the stories his prospects were telling themselves.

Their objections.

Their desires.

Their disbelief.

The thoughts and stories that many of them didn't even realize were holding them back (and keeping them from buying).

We spoke directly to his customers' hearts.

And they opened their wallets.

In that moment, I realized something that would change everything:

99% of service businesses are just one simple system away from a massive breakthrough.

But as with most discoveries, the path to that point wasn't straight...

Six months earlier, everything was falling apart.

It was my daughter's sixth birthday, and I was supposed to be celebrating with her at Build-A-Bear. Something she'd been talking about for months.

Instead, I was sitting in the passenger seat of our minivan in the mall parking lot, my phone buzzing non-stop with urgent messages from my business partner.

"Can you drive?" I asked my wife, not looking up from my screen. "I need to handle this right now."

She glanced over at me with **that** look. You know the one I'm talking about. The kind that says more than words ever could, especially when little ears are listening in the back seat.

Our four kids were all buckled in, excited to celebrate their sister's big day.

But I was drowning.

"Just give me a couple minutes," I asked my wife as she parked. "I'll be right in."

As entrepreneurs, we're used to dealing with fires.

But not all problems are created equal.

When I'm working with my team, I'm constantly training them to sort and filter the various problems we face.

Teaching them how to decide what's a priority and what's not is my top priority.

Is it a dumpster fire? Those usually burn themselves out if you leave them alone.

Or is it a kitchen fire? Those need immediate attention because they can take down the entire house.

This one.

The problem that showed up on my daughter's sixth birthday.

The one that had been slowly burning just below the surface for months.

Instantly turned into a full-blown kitchen fire.

And it was about to burn down everything I'd worked for.

I called my friend Matt. The only person I could trust to give it to me straight.

"I think I need to get out," I told him, pacing behind our van. "This thing is costing me my peace. It's costing me my family."

"What does your gut tell you?" he asked.

"That I should have left months ago."

"Then you have your answer."

I hung up, took a deep breath, and walked into Build-A-Bear.

My wife was helping our daughter pick an outfit for her birthday bear when I stepped into the store.

"We're leaving," I whispered to her.

"Today."

She looked up at me, and tears immediately filled her eyes.

"I'm so happy," she said, giving me the tightest hug I'd felt since our first dance the day of our wedding.

In that moment, I knew I'd made the right choice.

Within 3 short months, I moved my family from Bend, Oregon to Las Vegas, Nevada, back to Bend, Oregon, and finally to Nashville, Tennessee.

Which wasn't the original plan (obviously).

90 days. 3 states. 3,870 miles.

One family of six and everything we owned, frantically uprooted and searching for solid ground.

But somewhere between the U-Hauls and the uncertainty, I learned something that changed everything.

In fact, I had just learned the most important lesson of my life:

If something isn't worth the next 10 years of your life, it's not worth even 10 minutes of your attention.

And if I'm being honest, even though the circumstances were severe, the fresh start was exciting at first.

New city, new opportunities, endless possibilities.

But sometimes having too many options can be paralyzing.

And I knew that I couldn't afford to make the wrong next move.

So I did what felt right: I got still.

I spent 30 days journaling, hiking, and reflecting on what had gone wrong and what I wanted to build next.

I'd had success before:

- Spent my first 10 years in business as a professional photographer working with incredible clients around the world
- Helped scale a marketing agency to $25 million annually
- Launched a software company to over $140K monthly recurring revenue in less than 9 months

I had spent an entire decade (my 30's) leveling up and stacking wins. But now I was starting over.

About to turn 40 and resetting the clock.

And honestly? I was scared.

I had all this experience, all these skills, but I wasn't sure how to package all of it into something new. Something that would help a lot of people and make a lot of money.

Then I went on a guys' trip to Yosemite and everything changed.

That's where I met Cole.

Cole had a successful consulting business and was dealing with the exact same frustrations I'd helped solve with my previous companies.

Because solving marketing puzzles is what I do.

One of the final days of the trip, we were sitting around a fire pit after a long day hiking Half Dome when he started telling me about his marketing woes.

"I've done a few million in revenue," he said, "but I feel like I'm hitting a ceiling. I've tried agencies, bought programs, hired experts. Have had some success here and there, but nothing that really moves the needle like when I first started."

Something in his story felt familiar.

"What if the problem isn't your offer or your ads or your social media?" I posed.

"What if it's how you're handling the attention you've already got?"

His eyes lit up. "What do you mean?"

That conversation led to Cole hiring me to help dial in his marketing system.

Here's what Cole had going for him:

- ✅ Proven offer
- ✅ Happy clients
- ✅ Amazing testimonials
- ✅ And a track record of success

But he was stuck in the same trap most service businesses fall into...

Trying lots of different tactics instead of focusing on the constraint.

So first things first...

We identified his biggest bottleneck: the middle of his funnel.

More specifically, the people that had discovered Cole & his business but hadn't become a paying client (yet).

Cole was already posting a single short video to Instagram every day, and he was actually pretty good at it. So instead of starting from scratch, we doubled down on what was already working.

Every week, I'd meet with Cole and his team to plan his content strategy.

We put all our focus on creating a marketing system that spoke directly to the hearts and beliefs of his ideal customers.

We got really intentional about the conversation Cole was having with his audience, paying extra attention to the different stages people were at in their own personal journey.

We delivered messaging at scale, while making every message deeply personal.

Seven days later, my phone lit up with that text message.

Cole and his team were up late watching the final hours tick down on the deadline for the campaign.

As for me, I had already turned in for bed.

The next morning started like most of my days.

Coffee. Reading 10+ pages of a book. Breaking a sweat with my morning workout (#SweatEveryDay).

After toweling off and getting dressed I checked my phone for the first time. I'll never forget the moment I saw those numbers. We hadn't just improved his launch results. We had completely transformed his business.

$772,350 in sales.

Nearly four times his previous best launch.

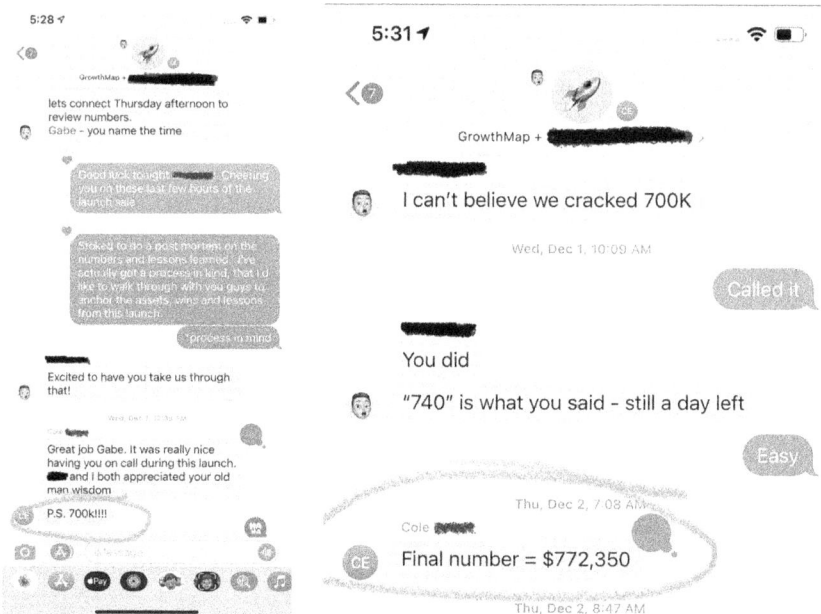

But here's what I learned from Cole's breakthrough and from helping 70+ other businesses scale: knowing WHAT to say once you have someone's attention and building a SYSTEM that makes it happen consistently are two different, but highly connected, things.

The Hook to Booked Blueprint™ shows you the optimal customer experience. It shows you exactly WHAT to do. What to say and how to say it.

The framework shows you how to systematically move people from stranger to buyer through four predictable stages.

This book is tactical. It will show you the blueprint.

And by the time you finish reading this book you'll know exactly what to do, and you'll have all the ingredients to install your own customer acquisition system that actually executes these tactics at scale.

Most business owners get stuck because they focus on one or the other.

They either know what should happen (the framework) but can't systemize it, or they build systems without understanding the customer experience those systems should deliver.

This book gives you both: the customer experience strategy AND the system requirements to execute it.

With Cole, he won big because he'd focused on one simple thing: **designing a customer experience** that spoke directly to his audience's disbelief and deepest needs at each stage of their individual journey.

That's when it hit me like a lightning bolt:

Most service business owners are spinning their wheels, bouncing between agencies and lead vendors, trying everything and mastering nothing.

But there's a timeless framework (one that's been around since the beginning of storytelling itself) that can turn even the most hesitant, skeptical prospects into eager buyers.

It's the same framework that every blockbuster movie follows.

The same framework that built empires and launched movements.

And it's the same framework that took Cole from a $200K launch to more than $772K in sales in just a few months.

In this book, I'm going to share that exact framework with you.

And if you want my personal help implementing it in your business, I'll show you the fastest way I know how to get your system up and running. But first, let's start with the blueprint your business needs.

The Hook to Booked Blueprint™ that turns strangers into hand-raisers, and hand-raisers into qualified, ready-to-buy clients.

Because here's what I've learned — and this is the fundamental truth that will transform your business:

You don't need more leads.

You don't need more followers.

You don't need more complicated funnels or expensive agencies.

You need more qualified conversations.

This isn't just marketing advice. This is how reality works. Like gravity. Like compound interest. Like every other immutable law that governs success.

Every business operates under this law whether they realize it or not. The businesses that thrive understand it. The ones that struggle fight against it.

And by the time you finish reading this book, you'll know exactly what to say to connect with the hearts of your best prospects. You'll have both the customer experience framework AND the system blueprint to implement it in your own business.

Let's get started.

PART I

THE FOUNDATION

The Universal Laws That Govern
Every Service Business

EXTERNAL	INTERNAL

CHAPTER 1

THE BUYER'S TIPPING POINT:
Why Timing Beats Everything

How to Be Top-of-Mind When Your Prospects' Pain Peaks

When 106 Million People Made the Same Decision at Once

July 20, 1969, 10:56 PM Eastern Time.

Neil Armstrong stepped onto the moon's surface, and 106 million Americans (nearly 60% of the entire U.S. population) watched it happen live on television.

All at the exact same moment.

This wasn't just history being made.

It was the last time an entire generation would share the same experience simultaneously.

And it reveals everything about why your best prospects are slipping through your fingers.

The Death of Captive Audiences

Back in 1969, if you wanted to reach people, it was simple.

There were three TV networks: ABC, NBC, and CBS.

That's it.

No cable, no streaming, no smartphones buzzing with notifications every 12 seconds.

If you wanted to advertise your business, you bought a 30-second spot during The Ed Sullivan Show, and BOOM! You had the attention of 60 million people.

You could literally **force yourself** to be top-of-mind.

Fast forward to today, and the average person sees over 5,000 advertisements per day.

We consume 34 GB of information daily. Enough to crash a laptop from the 1990s.

And we're being pulled in countless directions every waking moment.

The captive audience is dead.

And with it died the old way of doing business.

The Tony Robbins Moment

Which brings me to something I witnessed at a Tony Robbins event that changed how I think about marketing forever.

Tony was scanning the crowd of 8,000 people when he spotted a woman in the third row.

Tears streaming down her face.

He called her to stand up from her seat.

"What's going on?" he asked.

"I just got served divorce papers," she sobbed. "Lost my job last week. Just feel... completely broken."

The audience was silent.

Tony nodded.

His eyes filled with compassion.

He took a moment before he spoke and in an instant it felt like they were the only two people in the room.

You could hear a pin drop.

"Have you heard of me before today?"

"Yes," she said. "I've read your books. Listened to your talks. Watched your videos. For years."

"And why are you here now? Why didn't you take action before? What's different about today?"

She looked up at him with raw honesty.

"Because today... today... well... I just couldn't take it anymore. Couldn't take the pain. I finally had to do something about it."

7,999 people nodded in agreement.

Not because her story was unique.

But because every single person seated in that arena recognized themselves in that woman in that moment.

They all felt EXACTLY the same way.

The Universal Law of the Pain Clock

Here's what that woman taught me about human behavior.

That moment wasn't about logic.

It wasn't about persuasion.

It wasn't about overcoming objections.

It was about **timing**.

Tony just happened to be the one in front of her when her pain peaked.

And because she already trusted him, because he'd been consistently showing up in her world, she acted.

This is what I call the **Buyer's Tipping Point Principle** — the first immutable law every service provider must understand:

Buyer's Tipping Point Principle:

People buy when their pain peaks, from whoever is top-of-mind and trusted.

It doesn't matter if you have the best solution.

It doesn't matter if you're cheaper, faster, or more qualified.

If you're not top-of-mind and trusted when their tipping point hits, you lose to someone who is.

Even if your solution is objectively better.

The Most Important Conversation

But here's what most service providers miss about the tipping point moment.

There are always two conversations happening:

External Conversation: "I need help with this problem."

Internal Conversation: "Am I ready to admit I can't handle this myself? Can I trust this person? Will this actually work? What if I make the wrong choice?"

The Two Conversations

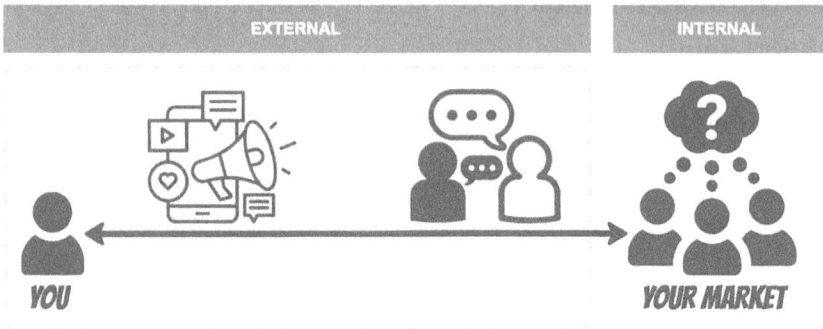

Your marketing. Your emails, social media, advertising and sales conversations — those are all the **External Conversations** that drive your business forward.

But the stories your market is telling themselves. The questions, objections, and subconscious disbelief your prospects aren't even aware of — those are all the **Internal Conversations** that the most successful entrepreneurs & leaders (like Tony Robbins) spend all of their time & energy to speak to.

The woman at Tony's event had been having the external conversation for years. She knew she needed help.

But the internal conversation was what kept her from taking action.

Until her pain became unbearable.

That's when the internal conversation shifted from "Do I need help?" to "I can't survive another day without help."

And Tony was there when it happened.

Emergency Rooms vs. Life Insurance

Some businesses have it easy.

If you're a tow truck driver, you never have to convince people their pain is unbearable.

When someone's car breaks down on the interstate at 11 PM, they're not comparison shopping.

They're grabbing the first trusted hand they can find. If that's you, hopefully you did the work ahead of time so you can be in the right place at the right time to scoop up a new customer and sell them your service.

But what if you sell life insurance?

Or dog training?

Or business consulting? Financial planning? Roofs? Custom cabinets?

Or any service where the pain isn't immediately obvious?

Your prospects might be bleeding internally for months before they realize they need help.

Your job becomes helping them recognize their own tipping point before it's too late.

Not through manipulation.

But by clarifying their problem better than they can articulate it themselves.

The Modern Attention Battlefield

Here's the challenge we face today.

In 1969, you could buy attention.

Plaster your message across three TV networks and millions of people had no choice but to see it.

Today, attention can't be bought. It must be earned.

Every day.

Every piece of content.

Every interaction.

Your prospects are living in a world with infinite options and zero patience.

The moment their pain peaks and they're ready to buy, they don't have time to research every option.

They grab the nearest trusted hand. **The question is: Will that be you?**

The Professional Credibility Principle

Here's what separates amateur service providers from true professionals:

Amateurs rely on hustle and hope. They post when they remember, follow up when they have time, and wonder why their results are inconsistent.

Professionals understand that credibility comes from reliability. Their prospects can count on valuable content, consistent communication, and professional follow-through.

In other words:

Professional credibility requires professional systems.

Think about the most successful entrepreneurs and service providers you know.

What do they all have in common?

- They show up consistently
- They follow proven processes
- They deliver predictable results

This isn't by accident. It's by design.

When your ideal client is ready to make a decision, they won't choose the person who "might" be there.

They'll choose the professional who has demonstrated reliability through consistent, valuable engagement.

What This Means for Your Business

The Buyer's Tipping Point changes everything about how you approach marketing.

You can't just run ads when you need more clients.

You can't just post on social media when you remember.

You can't just send an email when you have something to sell.

You need to be building trust and staying top-of-mind consistently, so you're positioned perfectly when your ideal prospect's pain peaks.

This isn't about being pushy.

It's about being present.

It isn't about adding more to your to-do list (you're already busy enough).

It's about consistently showing up in your prospect's world with helpful, valuable content that positions you as the trusted expert.

So when their pain finally peaks...

...when they hit their personal rock bottom...

...you're not a stranger trying to sell them something.

You're the obvious choice.

In the next chapter, we'll dive into the timeless framework that makes this possible — the same storytelling structure that's been used to captivate audiences for thousands of years, and how you can use it to speak directly to both conversations happening in your prospect's mind.

Because timing gets you in the door.

But story gets you the sale.

CHAPTER 2

THE HOLLYWOOD SECRET
That Sells Everything

Why Every Blockbuster Movie (and Successful Business) Follows the Same Timeless Story Formula

The $2.8 Billion Blockbuster Formula

What do Star Wars, Rocky, The Godfather, and Top Gun all have in common?

They've generated over $2.8 billion combined at the box office.

But that's not the real secret.

The real secret is that if you opened any of their screenplays to page 27, you'd find the exact same thing happening.

The hero meets their guide.

Luke meets Yoda. Rocky meets Mickey. Michael Corleone meets his father. Maverick meets Charlie.

Same page. Same moment. Same formula.

And that formula doesn't just sell movie tickets.

It sells everything.

The Discovery That Changed Hollywood Forever

In 1997, a screenwriting teacher named Robert McKee published a book called "Story" that revealed Hollywood's biggest secret... **the literal blueprint** behind every major blockbuster since Casablanca.

McKee had spent decades analyzing the most successful films in history, looking for patterns.

What he discovered was that every major motion picture, regardless of genre, budget, or decade, followed the exact same three-act structure:

Act 1: Setup (pages 1-30) - Introduce the hero in their ordinary world, then hit them with an inciting incident that forces them into action.

Act 2: Confrontation (pages 30-90) - The hero faces increasingly difficult obstacles while pursuing their goal, culminating in a crisis that seems impossible to overcome.

Act 3: Resolution (pages 90-120) - The hero finds the strength to overcome the final obstacle and emerges transformed.

But here's what McKee really discovered.

These weren't arbitrary rules created by Hollywood executives.

They were psychological principles hardwired into human nature.

Stories that follow this framework feel "right" to us because they mirror how we actually experience change and growth in our own lives.

Which is why this same framework that captivates audiences in darkened theaters can captivate your best prospects in your marketing.

My Freshman Year Revelation

During my freshman year in college, I studied radio, television, and film, dreaming of one day writing for Saturday Night Live.

Growing up, I'd made countless home movies with friends, always fascinated by what made some stories unforgettable and others... forgettable.

Then I took a screenwriting class that changed everything.

My professor assigned McKee's "Story" as required reading, and I became obsessed.

I started analyzing every movie I'd ever loved through McKee's framework. A group of my friends even started working through the AFI (American Film Institute) Top 100 movies.

Now I can't watch a movie without seeing this underlying pattern.

Star Wars: Luke's ordinary world gets destroyed (inciting incident), he trains with Yoda while battling the Empire (confrontation), then faces Vader and discovers his true identity (resolution).

Wicked: Elphaba starts as a misunderstood outsider trying to do good (ordinary world), discovers the Wizard's corruption and injustice (inciting incident), fights against the system while losing friends and reputation (confrontation), embraces her true power and finds her place as the champion of the oppressed (resolution).

Top Gun: Maverick: Maverick stuck in the past avoiding promotion (ordinary world), assigned an impossible mission (inciting incident), must train new pilots while confronting his own limitations and past trauma (confrontation), leads the successful mission and finally finds peace with his legacy (resolution).

The framework was everywhere.

But the real revelation came when my professor showed me that the best stories didn't just follow this structure on the surface.

They spoke to something deeper.

They articulated feelings and struggles that audiences couldn't quite put into words themselves.

They tapped into a subconscious frequency that made viewers feel something.

When Luke Skywalker stared at the twin suns of Tatooine, yearning for adventure, millions of people thought: "That's exactly how I feel about my life."

When Elphaba sang about being misunderstood and different, millions of viewers thought: "That's exactly how I feel when people don't get me."

These stories worked because they clarified problems better than the audience could articulate themselves.

And that's when it hit me.

This wasn't just about entertainment.

This was about connection.

This was about understanding.

This was about trust.

The Mentor's Lesson That Changed Everything

Years later, I was newly engaged and eager to connect with my fiancée while building my side hustle into a full-time business.

So I asked my mentor a critical question:

"How do I grow my business and be an amazing husband? I haven't done either one yet."

My mentor (his name is Dane) sat back and smiled.

He thought for a moment before giving me the answer that would transform how I understand human communication.

"There are always two conversations happening at any given time," he explained.

"There's the external conversation out in the open. The one we're having right now."

"And then there's the internal conversation. The one happening in your head right now... at the exact same time... ABOUT the conversation out in the open."

I didn't understand what these two conversations had to do with being a successful entrepreneur and a great husband.

My mentor could tell I needed more detail, so he continued.

"The words that we are exchanging back and forth... this first conversation is where most new husbands focus their attention..."

What did she just say...

How should I respond...

"And in the same way, it's this first conversation where most struggling entrepreneurs focus. They spend all their time and energy..."

Improving their pitch...

Working on their marketing...

Refining the message to share with their market.

"But the SECOND conversation..."

He leaned forward.

"That internal conversation. The unspoken story your wife is telling herself. The one inside the mind of your best customers."

"**That** is the one to pay attention to."

The Two Conversations in Action

Think about it.

When your spouse texts you from work, "We need to talk," there are two conversations happening.

Conversation #1 (External): "We need to talk."

Conversation #2 (Internal): "What did I do wrong? Are they unhappy with me? Is this about money? The kids? Are they thinking about leaving? How serious is this? Should I be worried?"

That internal conversation — those beliefs, those feelings, those unspoken fears — that's what determines how you respond and how the entire conversation unfolds.

And the exact same thing happens with your marketing.

When you send an email to a new lead about your services, there are two conversations happening.

Conversation #1 (External): "Here's how me and my team can help you."

Conversation #2 (Internal): "Do they actually understand what I'm going through? Have they dealt with someone in my exact situation before? Can I trust them with this? Are they just trying to sell me something, or do they genuinely want to help? Is it worth it? Do I have the time for this?"

The Doctor's Diagnosis Principle

Here's a perfect example of speaking to the internal conversation.

Imagine you go to a doctor because you've been feeling tired and achy for weeks. You know something is wrong, but you don't know what.

You schedule an appointment with your family doctor, but decide to book a second consultation with another doc just to be safe and get a different opinion.

Doctor A says: "Once you've filled out your paperwork and answered the intake questionnaire, we'll run a few tests to see what's wrong."

Doctor B says: "Before we run any tests, can you confirm a couple things for me? Based on what you're describing, I'm guessing you're waking up around 3 AM feeling anxious, you're craving carbs in the afternoon, and you probably feel like your brain is in a fog most days. Sound about right?"

Which doctor do you trust more?

Doctor B, obviously.

Not because they've diagnosed you yet.

Not because they've prescribed a treatment.

But because they demonstrated that they understand your problem better than you could articulate it yourself.

You hadn't actually thought about it until they said so, but you had been craving carbs more than usual, and you're going on day 3 of waking up between 3-4 AM with restless thoughts.

It was as if Doctor B had been right there beside you the whole time, knowing exactly what was going on.

In that moment, you automatically assume they have the solution.

This is what it means to trust your gut.

Because your gut trusts the expert that best understands your problem.

The Authority Marketing Advantage

Traditional advertising interrupts people to get attention.

Authority marketing earns attention by providing value first.

And value always follows empathy.

When Doctor B demonstrated understanding of the patient's exact symptoms, they weren't advertising their services. They were demonstrating their authority through empathy.

This is the difference between ineffective interruption-based marketing (spammy ads, cold calls, direct mail) and authority-based marketing (valuable content that positions you as the expert).

Authority Marketing beats traditional advertising 10 times out of 10.

Your prospects are already being bombarded with traditional ads.

But when you speak to their internal conversation with doctor-like precision, you're not competing with other advertisers...

You're establishing yourself as the trusted authority they've been searching for.

The Most Important Principle in Marketing

Here's the truth that separates amateur marketers from professionals:

"Get intimately familiar with the conversation going on inside the mind of your best customers, and you'll never run out of qualified leads to sell and serve."

Because conversions can only happen in conversation.

When you can articulate your market's problem better than they can, something magical happens.

You don't just become another service provider trying to sell them something.

You become the person who "gets it."

You become the obvious choice.

You become the trusted brand they've been searching for.

You enter a different conversation (literally) in the mind of your prospect.

But how do you actually do this systematically?

How do you speak to both conversations in your marketing consistently?

The answer lies in the same storytelling framework that's been captivating audiences for thousands of years.

The Universal Story Structure

Every compelling story follows the same basic pattern:

1. **Hero in their ordinary world** (your prospect's current situation)
2. **Inciting incident** (the problem that forces them to seek help)
3. **Meeting the guide** (discovering you and your solution)
4. **Facing challenges** (working through objections and obstacles)
5. **Transformation** (achieving their desired outcome)

This structure works because it mirrors your prospect's actual journey from problem to solution.

When your marketing follows this same pattern, it feels natural and trustworthy to your prospects because it matches their internal experience.

What This Means for Your Content

Every piece of content you create should address both conversations.

Surface level (External Conversation): Here's what I can do for you.

Deeper level (Internal Conversation): Here's what I understand about your world that others miss.

When your prospect consumes your content and thinks, "This person understands my situation better than I do," you've won.

Not because you've made the best logical argument.

But because you've created an emotional connection based on understanding.

And understanding, more than anything else, creates **trust**.

In the next chapter, we'll explore the critical factor that can make or break even the most perfectly crafted message: timing. You'll discover why you have exactly 60 seconds to capitalize on that perfect moment when trust meets opportunity, and what happens when you miss that window.

Because story creates the connection.

But speed determines who gets the sale.

CHAPTER 3

MONEY LOVES SPEED:
The 60-Second Window That Makes or Breaks Your Business

Why Speed-to-Lead Determines Who Gets the Deal (and How to Win Every Time)

Five minutes.

That's how long you have.

After that, your chances of winning the prospect drop by more than 80%.

After an hour? You might as well delete their contact information.

Yet the average service business takes 47 hours to respond to a new lead.

Which explains why one of Alex Hormozi's friends pays someone $80,000 a year to work just 10 minutes per day.

And it's the smartest money he's ever spent.

The Most Expensive Phone Call You'll Never Make

Alex was having coffee with a friend who runs a successful service business.

They were talking about hiring and operational efficiency when his friend mentioned something that made Alex nearly spit out his drink.

"I pay Sarah $80,000 a year," his friend said casually.

"And what exactly does she do?" Alex asked.

"She calls every lead back within five minutes."

Alex leaned forward. "You must get a ton of leads to justify that kind of salary."

"Actually, no. We get maybe two to five leads per day."

Alex did the math in his head.

Five leads per day, maybe two minutes per call.

That's 10 minutes of actual work.

For $80,000 a year.

"Are you insane?" Alex asked.

His friend smiled. "Best investment I've ever made. That $80,000 salary pays for itself 10 times over."

"How?"

"Because the day I miss even one lead... the day I let one slip through the cracks because I was too busy to call back immediately... I lose a $15,000 client."

"And when I was handling it myself, I was missing at least one or two leads every week."

The math was staggering.

Missing just two leads per week cost him over $1.5 million annually.

Paying Sarah $80,000 to prevent that?

A no-brainer.

The Science of Disappearing Opportunities

Here's what most service business owners don't understand about lead response time.

Every minute that passes after someone reaches out, your chances of conversion drop dramatically.

Studies show that **calling a lead within the first minute gives you a 391% higher chance of conversion** compared to calling within the first hour.

Within five minutes? You're still 100 times more likely to connect than if you wait 30 minutes.

After an hour? You might as well not call at all.

But here's the part that will shock you.

The average service business takes 47 hours to respond to a new lead.

47 hours.

By then, your prospect has not only moved on. They've probably already hired your competitor.

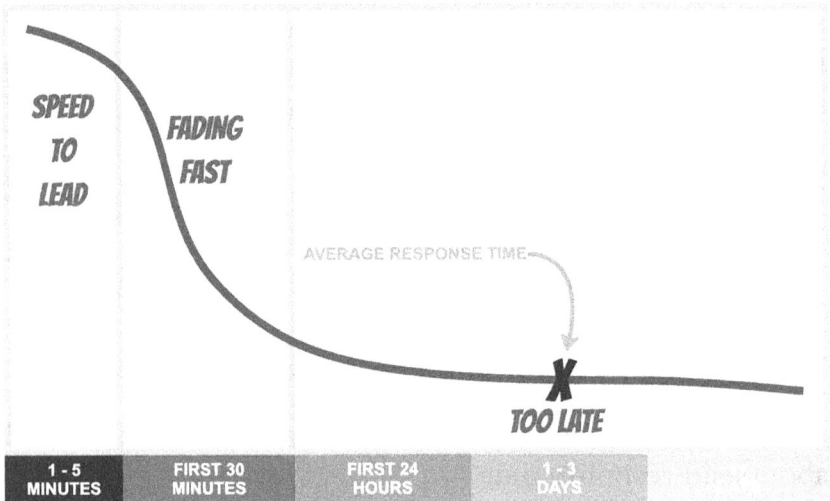

The 2 Convos During the First 5 Minutes

Remember what we learned about the two conversations happening in every interaction?

When someone fills out your contact form or responds to your ad, there are two conversations racing through their mind:

External Conversation: "I submitted my information. Now I wait for them to get back to me."

Internal Conversation: "Did I make the right choice? Are they going to call me right away? What if they don't call back? Maybe I should try someone else. I wonder if that other company would be able to help me faster… oh shoot… need to respond to that email…" (attention exits stage left)

That internal conversation is a ticking time bomb.

Every minute you delay, doubt creeps in. Second-guessing intensifies. The urgency that drove them to reach out begins to fade. Attention diminishes.

But when you respond within 60 seconds?

External Conversation: "Wow, they called back already."

Internal Conversation: "These people are serious. They actually care about helping me. They must be good at what they do if they're this responsive. I'm dealing with professionals."

Speed doesn't just capture attention. It transforms the internal conversation from doubt to trust.

The Susie and Teddy Breakthrough

Which brings me to Susie and Teddy, who run a dog training business.

Susie is one of those business owners who wears 47 different hats.

She's got a daughter in college, another child at home with special needs, and she's trying to run a business that actually helps people.

Oh yeah... and Susie doesn't have just one business.

She has two.

In addition to working with families and their furry friends with her business partner Teddy, she also manages the family business, a brick and mortar garden center that's been well established in their community for decades.

Before working with us, Susie knew speed-to-lead was important.

She did her best to get back to prospects quickly.

But "quickly" meant 30 minutes if she was lucky.

An hour if she was with another client.

And weekends? Forget about it.

Family has always been top priority for Susie, so everything waited until Monday morning.

Susie was losing deals left and right... a slow but obvious leak in her marketing & sales... and she knew it.

But what could she do?

She couldn't be glued to her phone 24/7.

She had a life. A family. Other clients to serve.

The breakthrough came when she installed a system that solved the speed-to-lead problem once and for all.

Now every single lead that comes into her dog training business gets a response within 60 seconds.

24/7/365.

No exceptions.

Within 90 days of installing this system, Susie tripled her sales.

From $20,000 per month to over $64,000.

All because she stopped missing the attention window.

The Midnight Epiphany

A few months after implementing the system, Susie called me with excitement in her voice.

"You're not going to believe what just happened," she said.

"Two people scheduled demos at 2 AM last night. They must have been browsing our site late, couldn't sleep, and decided to reach out."

"And here's the crazy part... I know for a fact that if it were just up to me to respond, they never would have scheduled."

"By the time I would have called them back at 8 or 9 AM the next day, they would have already moved on to someone else or probably just ignored my calls."

"But because our system responded instantly, they're both on my calendar for this week."

That's when it hit me.

This isn't just about business hours.

Your prospects don't operate on your schedule.

They operate on theirs.

And their schedule might be 2 AM on a Tuesday.

When their pain peaks at midnight, when their frustration boils over during a weekend, when their tipping point hits on a holiday — that's when they reach out.

If you're not there to catch them in that moment, someone else will be.

The Emergency Room Principle

Think about this for a second.

If you're having a heart attack, do you call the hospital and leave a voicemail?

Do you send an email and wait for a response?

Of course not.

You call 911, and someone answers immediately.

Because in emergencies, every second counts.

Here's the thing: when your prospect reaches out, it IS an emergency to them.

Their pain has finally peaked.

They've hit their tipping point.

They're ready to solve their problem right now.

Not tomorrow.

Not next week.

Right now.

If you're not there to catch them in that moment, someone else will be.

The Foundation Principle

Here's the truth that separates thriving businesses from struggling ones.

Money loves speed.

In the game of leads, speed beats everything, including price, quality, and experience.

This is another immutable law that governs every service business:

Your prospect isn't looking for the best solution when they reach out.

They're looking for the fastest solution from someone they trust.

If you can be both fast AND trustworthy, you win.

Every time.

Remember: People buy when their pain peaks, from whoever is top-of-mind and trusted.

But if you're not fast enough to catch them at their tipping point, it doesn't matter how much they trust you.

Someone else will be there instead.

The 24/7/365 Solution

Now, I know what you're thinking.

"This sounds great, but I can't be available 24/7 without sacrificing my personal life."

You're absolutely right.

And you don't have to be.

The solution isn't working more hours. It's building a system that responds instantly even when you're sleeping, spending time with family, or serving other clients.

Because automated systems create consistency at scale.

Just like Susie's dog training business, the most successful professional service providers understand that consistency beats intensity. You can't personally respond to every lead within 60 seconds, but a well-designed system can.

This is especially critical for financial advisors, contractors, event planners and other professional service providers where trust and timing are everything.

Your prospects don't care that it's 10 PM on a Sunday. Their pain peaks when it peaks.

The businesses that capture these moments are the ones that have systems working for them around the clock.

What This Means for Your Business

Speed-to-lead isn't just a nice-to-have anymore.

It's table stakes.

If you're not responding to leads within 60 seconds, you're not just losing individual deals.

You're systematically bleeding revenue.

Every day.

Every week.

Every month.

The good news?

This is completely fixable.

And when you fix it, the results are immediate and dramatic.

Just ask Susie, who tripled her sales in 90 days. Or Alex's friend, who turned an $80,000 investment into over $1.5 million in saved revenue.

The question isn't whether you can afford to solve this problem.

The question is whether you can afford not to.

In the next chapter, we'll expose the biggest lie that's been bankrupting service businesses for decades. You'll discover why everything you've been told about lead generation is wrong, and what to focus on instead.

Because now that you understand WHY people buy, HOW to speak to their internal conversation, and WHEN to catch them at their tipping point...

It's time to reveal WHAT most businesses get completely backwards about growth so you can do the opposite... and win big.

CHAPTER 4

THE LEAD GENERATION LIE
That's Bankrupting Service Businesses

Why Chasing More Leads Is Keeping You Broke (and What to Do Instead)

Now that you understand the fundamental laws governing every service business — why timing beats everything, how story sells everything, and why speed determines who wins — it's time to expose the biggest lie destroying businesses today.

The lie that's bankrupting 91% of service businesses isn't that they need better products or lower prices.

It's that they think they need more leads.

Which they don't.

They need a better system.

The 50,000 Lead Traffic Boost That Generated Zero Sales

What if I told you that 50,000 qualified prospects visited a company's online store every month, and the owner still went broke?

You'd probably think I was lying.

But that's exactly what happened to one of my business partners' old clients, and it perfectly illustrates why everything you've been told about lead generation is backwards.

They sold lancets (those tiny needles diabetics use to test blood sugar). Great product, massive market, obvious need.

When they hired my partner's company, their website was getting maybe 5,000 visitors per month at best.

"We just need more traffic," the owner said. "If we can get more diabetics to our site, we'll make more sales."

Classic thinking, right? More leads equals more sales.

So the team went to work. Researched what diabetics cared about. What they were searching. What problems they needed solved.

Within nine months, they had more than 50,000 unique visitors hitting their website every month. Ten times more traffic than when the project started.

The owner should have been celebrating.

Instead, he was furious.

Because despite all that traffic, revenue barely moved.

They had poured 50,000 qualified prospects into a leaky bucket.

Their website looked nice, but it didn't give visitors a compelling reason to buy. No clear value proposition. No way to capture contact information. No follow-up system for people who weren't ready to purchase immediately.

They had solved the wrong problem.

The Assembly Line Revolution Reveals the Real Problem

In 1913, Henry Ford did something that changed the world forever.

But it wasn't what most people think.

Everyone assumes Ford's genius was inventing the car or even the assembly line itself. They're wrong.

Ford didn't invent the automobile. He perfected the system that made cars affordable and scalable.

Ford's breakthrough was understanding that efficiency came not from getting more parts, but from fixing the constraints in production flow.

Before Ford, car manufacturing was chaos. Cars were made by hand, one at a time. It took forever, cost a fortune, and only rich people could afford cars.

Ford looked at this broken system and asked a different question.

Instead of "How do we build cars faster?" he asked "What's preventing us from building cars faster?"

The answer wasn't more parts or more workers. **It was the system itself**.

So Ford redesigned everything. He broke car manufacturing into simple, repeatable steps. He positioned workers strategically along a moving assembly line. He identified and eliminated every bottleneck that slowed production.

The result? Ford could turn raw materials into finished Model T's faster and cheaper than anyone else in the world.

By 1927, Ford had sold over 15 million Model T's and transformed America from an agricultural society into an industrial powerhouse.

All because he focused on the system, not just the inputs.

The Theory of Constraints in Your Business

Here's why most service business owners stay stuck.

They don't understand one of the most important principles in business:

Theory of Constraints: A system is only as effective as its weakest link.

You can have the best advertising in the world, but if your follow-up system is broken, you'll waste every dollar. You can be amazing at converting leads to sales, but if you can't attract enough prospects, you'll starve. You can create incredible content, but if it doesn't move people to take action, you're just entertainment.

This is why so many service businesses live on the revenue roller coaster. Great month, terrible month, okay month, disaster month.

They keep trying to solve their sales problem by pouring more leads into a broken system.

It's like trying to fill a bucket with holes in the bottom. The solution isn't a bigger hose. It's fixing the holes.

The Two Systems Every Business Needs

Every successful marketing system consists of exactly two sub-systems working in harmony:

1: Capture System — How you capture attention from the right people with the right message at the right time.

2: Conversion System — How you convert that attention into qualified conversations and paying clients.

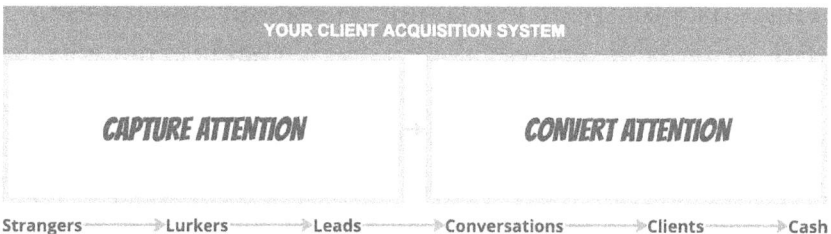

YOUR CLIENT ACQUISITION SYSTEM	
CAPTURE ATTENTION	**CONVERT ATTENTION**

Strangers ···▶ Lurkers ···▶ Leads ···▶ Conversations ···▶ Clients ···▶ Cash

Most service businesses fail because they're missing something in one or both systems.

They either get great at attracting attention but can't convert it into conversations. Or they're excellent at converting but can't attract enough prospects in the first place.

Success requires both systems working together as designed.

But what's the straw that stirs the drink?

It's not the system itself. It's the experience that system creates.

The experience every prospect has from the moment they discover you to the moment they hire you.

Which is exactly what the Hook to Booked Blueprint™ reveals — the 4 stages that transform reluctant strangers into eager buyers.

The Foundation Principle That Changes Everything

Here's the truth that will transform your business:

You don't need more leads. You need more qualified conversations.

This isn't just about marketing. It's about understanding that sustainable growth comes from systems, not tactics. From fixing constraints, not adding inputs. From creating qualified prospects who are primed and ready to buy, not just collecting more names in your database and trying to convince them to buy.

Because here's what I've learned after helping 300+ busi-nesses scale: amateurs simply "work" the leads in their pipeline, while professionals **create** demand out of thin air.

And they do that by cultivating a specific experience for every person who discovers their business.

An experience that moves people systematically from stranger to buyer through four predictable stages — regardless of whether they're ready to buy immediately or need time to develop trust.

What Comes Next

You've laid the foundation and now you've got the strategic principles you need to grow your business.

Congrats!

You're already ahead of 80% of business owners. Most have no clue about these principles.

Now it's time to put you in the top 1% and show you how to apply them.

It's time to get tactical.

In the following chapters, we'll build your Hook to Booked experience step by step. You'll learn exactly how to identify the biggest constraint in your current marketing and sales process.

How to create a system that attracts the right attention and converts it into qualified conversations.

How to turn strangers into followers, followers into leads, leads into conversations, and conversations into clients who refer others (we call this your Freedom Flywheel™).

But first, you needed to understand this fundamental truth: The businesses that thrive understand that connection beats collection. Conversation beats conquest. Relationship beats reach.

Because that's where sales happen.

In connection.

In conversation.

In relationship.

Whether you sell 1-to-1 like Susie.

Or 1-to-many like Cole.

When you build the system. The system builds the business.

And that's exactly what we're going to build together.

But if you're impatient (like me) and you already know you need this system in your business, would it be okay if I shared a shortcut with you real quick?

Now, I know we've only just begun…

…and I haven't shared every detail of the system just yet

…but if you'd like the shortcut, the best way I know how to get your system working for you asap is by doing it live together.

Which is why I'd like to invite you to my next workshop.

You can get all the details at **HookToBooked.com/workshop**

Dates & seats are limited, so check the link to see if there are still spots available.

Register right now to secure your spot. And then continue reading.

Because now that you understand the universal laws, you're ready to learn the 4-stage system that puts them into action.

PART II

THE FOUR-STAGE SYSTEM

The Blueprint That Turns
Strangers into Buyers

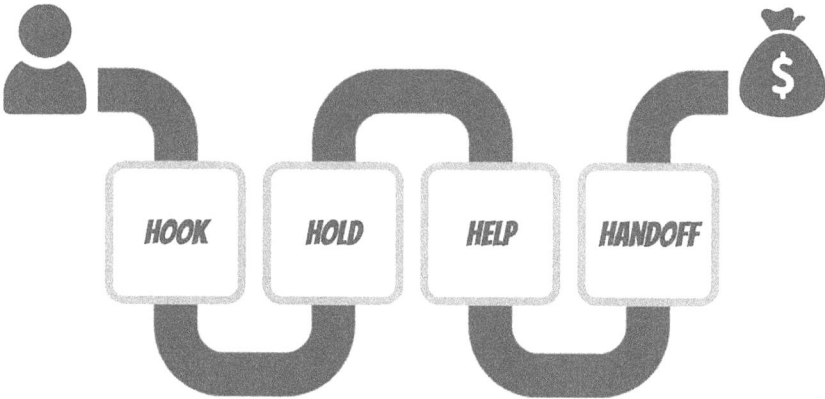

CHAPTER 5

THE HOOK:
The 3-Second Rule

How to Create Attention-Grabbing Content That Makes Prospects Pause and Pay Attention

The Invisible Leak in Your Business

Right now (as you read these very words) your best potential clients are flowing past your business like an underground river.

You can't see them. You can't count them. But they are there.

Every single day, qualified prospects who desperately need exactly what you offer are scrolling past your content, visiting your website, talking to your clients, driving past you, seeing your ads... and moving on.

Without stopping. Without engaging. Without raising their hand.

Each one represents money flowing straight out the door.

Because no matter how good your service is, how much experience you have, or how desperately someone needs your help...

If you can't stop the scroll, you can't make the sale.

The businesses that thrive have mastered one critical skill: they know how to create a pattern interrupt that makes the right people pause and pay attention.

They've learned to fish in the flowing river of attention instead of trying to create their own pond.

And it all starts with The Hook.

But what exactly is a hook?

A hook is something that grabs your prospect's attention and creates an irresistible need to know more.

It elicits a burning question (even better if it is more than one burning question) that they feel they **must** answer, and because of that burning question, they pay attention to you.

They stop. They engage. They want to know more.

It's the difference between being invisible and being impossible to ignore.

The Dear Sophie Revolution

In 2011, Google did something that struck a nerve with millions of people. Something that most of that year's best Hollywood films couldn't.

They created a 90-second commercial that made grown adults cry.

Not because they talked about email features or explained their technology or offered a discount.

But because they captured people's attention in the first three seconds and never let go.

The ad opened with a father creating a new Gmail account: dear.sophie.lee@gmail.com.

Then a new email: *Dear Sophie, You arrived!*

A single photo appears. A proud new dad holding his baby girl.

I am still getting the hang of holding you...

Click. Send.

In just six seconds, they hit a nerve that every parent in the world could feel. The curiosity gap opened instantly: "What's going to happen next? Who will little Sophie become?"

For the next 84 seconds, you watched Sophie grow up through her father's emails. First birthday. Becoming a big sister. Getting sick. Family vacations. Losing teeth. Dance recitals.

Each email creating a new hook, a new moment you **needed** to see.

Until the final message: *I can't wait to share these with you one day. Until then... Love, Dad*

By the end, millions of viewers were emotionally invested in this family they'd never met.

Google never mentioned storage space, spam filters, or technical features.

They simply mastered the hook.

That single ad generated over 100 million views and became one of the most successful campaigns in Google's history.

My Client's $2 Million Lesson

But you don't need a Super Bowl budget to master the hook.

Let me tell you about Jodi.

Jodi was a wedding photographer with a problem. She was incredibly talented, but she couldn't get clients.

All her photographer friends were younger and naturally connected to people getting engaged. Jodi was older (not much older btw), married with kids, and her friend group had moved past the wedding phase.

"I don't know where to find engaged couples," she told me. "Everyone I know is already married or having babies."

"Where do you think engaged couples hang out?" I asked.

We brainstormed and landed on the obvious answer: bridal fairs.

"Oh no," Jodi said. "Those are just meat markets for price shoppers. That's not my ideal client."

"But that's where the brides are," I replied. "You just need to learn how to hook their attention differently than everyone else."

Reluctantly, Jodi agreed to try a bridal fair. Just one... as a test.

She focused on creating genuine connections instead of competing on price, and ended up booking just a few clients from the event. Nothing life-changing. Just enough to get started.

But here's where it gets interesting.

Jodi did such an amazing job with those few clients that they became her referral engine.

Within two years, she became one of the most sought-after wedding photographers in the country. The best wedding planners and venues wanted Jodi working their events.

She photographed celebrities, luxury weddings, and even ended up shooting the wedding of a Chicago Cubs all-star during their 2016 World Series championship season.

From struggling to find a single client to photographing million-dollar weddings.

All because she learned to position herself where her ideal clients were already hanging out and mastered the art of capturing their attention.

The wedding world was one weekend away from never experiencing what Jodi had to offer.

But Jodi put in the work to connect with the people she was meant to serve.

Today? The student has become the teacher and Jodi works with clients & photographers all over the world, showing them how to capture attention.

Traffic Is Like a River

Think of attention like a flowing river.

A continual stream of people. Your best future clients. Flowing past your business every single day.

The river is always flowing. There's never a shortage.

Your job isn't to create the river. It's to position yourself in the flow and learn how to catch what you need.

Most service business owners make two critical mistakes:

Mistake #1: They try to create their own river (building an audience from scratch).

Mistake #2: They stand in the right river but use terrible bait (boring, generic content).

The traffic already exists.

Your ideal clients are already on social media, at events, consuming content online, engaging with other people's posts, and buying from someone else.

You don't need to create attention. You need to capture it.

But how?

H.O.O.K. 'Em: The Four-Step Framework

Over the years, I've invested over $200,000 in masterminds, coaching, and personal development.

Most of the time, the frameworks and strategies make the investment worthwhile. But there's one thing that always gives me an ROI: the people I meet.

Because broke people don't invest in their growth. Winners do.

Last year, I hired a new coach. My $9,000 investment paid for itself in less than 15 minutes after meeting Adley.

Adley is the woman behind some of the most viral content on the internet. She's personally responsible for billions of views for herself, her creators, and the companies they partner with.

During one of our group coaching calls, she opened up and shared the secret to her content success – the recipe she used to fill her wall with Gold and Silver YouTube play buttons.

She told us: "Create an itch in the first 3 seconds that you don't scratch until the last 3 seconds."

BOOM. It clicked instantly.

What Adley shared unlocked something I had seen over the past decade but hadn't noticed the pattern. After working with hundreds of clients and analyzing thousands of pieces of content, every great hook follows the same four-step formula:

H - Hit the Nerve

Your opening must strike a specific pain point or problem in 3 seconds or less.

Not a general problem. A specific one that makes your ideal client think: "That's exactly what I'm dealing with."

O - Open the Curiosity Gap

Make them care about what happens next. Give them a reason to keep reading, keep watching, stop scrolling.

Create a gap between what they know and what they want to know.

Shock value alone isn't enough. It must lead somewhere valuable.

O - Offer a New Possibility

Present a fresh perspective, insight, or idea they haven't considered.

This doesn't mean contradicting their beliefs. It means giving them language for something they already feel but couldn't articulate.

K - Keep Them Hooked

The best hooks lead to more hooks.

Pay off the curiosity gap you created, but immediately open a new gap that pulls them deeper into your world.

Think TV cliffhangers, but with substance.

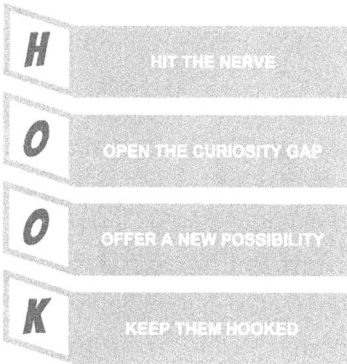

H HIT THE NERVE

O OPEN THE CURIOSITY GAP

O OFFER A NEW POSSIBILITY

K KEEP THEM HOOKED

WHAT IS A HOOK?

Something that grabs your prospect's attention and creates an irresistible need to know more.

Before You Make the Sale, You've Got to Stop the Scroll

Here's the truth that separates content that converts from content that gets ignored:

Every piece of content you create has one job before it can do anything else: catch someone's attention.

Before you can educate, you must capture attention.

Before you can persuade, you must create curiosity.

Before you can convert, you must connect.

And connection starts with a hook that makes someone pause and think: "What's this all about?"

This is why the Google "Dear Sophie" ad worked. This is why Jodi's authentic approach at bridal fairs worked. This is why Adley's content gets billions of views.

They all understood that in today's attention economy, you have approximately three seconds to prove you're worth someone's time. Miss that window, and they're gone forever.

What This Means for Your Content

Every piece of content you create should start with the H.O.O.K. framework:

1. **Hit the nerve** with your opening line, subject line, or first 3 seconds
2. **Open the curiosity gap** immediately after hitting the nerve
3. **Offer a new possibility** that reframes their problem or solution
4. **Keep them hooked** by creating anticipation for what comes next

Every email. Every ad. Every text message. Every video. Every post.

Remember: the goal isn't to be shocking for shock's sake. It's got to be genuinely interesting and helpful in a way that demands attention.

When someone sees your content and thinks, "I need to see where this goes," you've created a hook. When they can't scroll past without engaging, you've mastered the art. But stopping the scroll is just the beginning. Because you can't grow your business unless you **keep** their attention once you've caught it.

Which is exactly what we'll cover in the next chapter: The Hold.

You'll learn exactly how to turn that initial attention into genuine engagement and move prospects from casual viewers to active participants in your sales process.

Because stopping the scroll is just the first step.

Now you need to prove you're worth their time.

CHAPTER 6

THE HOLD:
Proof of Life Protocol

How to Get More People to Raise Their Hand, Reach Out, and Take Themselves Off the Market

---

The First Question That Changes Everything

What if I told you that a single simple question, shared with your prospect within the first 3-5 minutes of them reaching out, could double or triple your revenue?

Not by getting twice as many leads.

Not by improving your close rate.

But by just getting more people to actually respond when you reach out.

The Airport Discovery

Picture this: You're walking through the airport with your spouse, about to go on an incredible island vacation you've been planning for over a year.

You've made it through security and have time before your flight. Your spouse wants to grab water and snacks, so you duck into a Hudson News.

While they head to the fridge, you wander to the book section. You already know what you're looking for. Maybe a business book to fuel your entrepreneurial mind, or fiction from your favorite author.

As you scan the shelves, most books look remarkably similar. White covers with black text. Black covers with white text. Neutral beiges and grays. Boring titles. Nothing stands out.

But then one book catches your eye.

Bright orange cover that practically jumps off the shelf. Intriguing title that seems like exactly what you're looking for.

So you grab it. Flip to the back cover, then open to the table of contents.

That's when you discover this book is about Pythagoras, the Greek mathematician from 500 BC.

Unless you're secretly passionate about ancient geometry, this isn't what you had in mind.

You put the book back and return to scanning when your spouse appears with snacks and water.

You head to your gate empty-handed.

The Hidden Problem Most Businesses Never See

Here's what that airport story reveals about your business.

The bright orange book cover worked perfectly. It stopped your scroll. Grabbed your attention.

But the moment you opened it and realized it wasn't relevant to what you were looking for, you put it back.

The same thing happens to your prospects every single day.

Your content hooks their attention. They respond to your ad, visit your website, download your freebie, or fill out your contact form.

But then they disappear.

They ghost.

Not because your offer isn't good. Not because they don't need what you provide.

But because you never gave them a compelling reason to engage beyond their initial interest.

The Universal Truth

This principle applies everywhere:

Netflix doesn't just get you to start watching a show — they engineer the first episode to make you immediately want episode two.

Costco doesn't just put products on shelves — they strategically place sample stations to get you engaging with products you'd never otherwise try.

Apple doesn't just make phones — they design the unboxing experience to create an emotional moment that deepens your connection to the brand.

The pattern is universal: capture attention, then immediately convert that attention into engagement.

The $73,000 Website Banner

A couple years ago, I was working with a well-known software company in the digital marketing space that was serving a few thousand creators and was making a few million bucks a year.

But they were stuck. They had hit a ceiling with their sales.

So they hired me to help increase revenue.

In my research, I realized they had good website traffic and a solid system for getting people to sign up for free trials. But that was it.

The only way they were turning visitors into leads was by committing to a full trial of their software.

But there was a big opportunity in something you and I both know to be true. I didn't need to go generate any traffic & leads. The traffic was already there.

I just needed to help them find a way to capture it.

So I created a simple free resource that solved a pressing problem for their market. Then I added a single line of text at the top of their site inviting visitors to get the free guide.

A single subtle banner that said "Get the FREE Ultimate Offer Blueprint."

That was it.

As soon as we went live, the company started getting 20-30 new leads per day from that one little tweak.

Every day.

So I did the math.

This company had run paid ads in the past with an average cost per lead of about $10 each. By capturing 20+ leads per day, I calculated that those new "free" leads would be worth at least $73,000 per year in ad spend.

In other words: What would have cost them $73,000... they got absolutely free.

Because once we had their attention, we figured out how to get people to engage. And those leads would be worth even more when they turned into paying customers.

Here's the kicker: These were leads that **had been flowing right past them all along**. The business just hadn't given them a reason to raise their hand.

The Proof of Life Protocol

Here's the truth that separates thriving businesses from struggling ones:

You don't need more leads. You need more qualified conversations.

Your perfect customers are already out there. They're already flowing past your business like that underground river we talked about.

Some are even raising their hands and expressing interest.

But here's where most businesses fail: they confuse **interest** with **engagement**.

Interest is someone responding to your ad. **Engagement** is that same someone texting you back right away.

Interest is someone filling out your contact form. **Engagement** is that same someone replying to your intro email.

Interest gets you their attention. Engagement gets you their trust.

And trust is what converts to sales.

The Two-Step Protocol

So how do the most successful service providers and entrepreneurs hold attention and engage new leads?

They do two simple things. On purpose. With every single lead.

Step 1: Give them a reason to raise their hand

This is where Fly Trap Offers™ come in.

Unlike generic lead magnets that try to appeal to everyone, Fly Trap Offers™ are laser-focused on one specific problem your ideal client is facing right now.

Think single-serving size. Like the two-Advil packet you grab at a gas station when you have a headache.

It solves one specific problem in 5-10 minutes and creates a clear bridge to your larger solution.

But how do you package up your Fly Trap Offers™?

Make it easy to consume. The 5 best packages to deliver your single-serving solution: a guide, a template, a tool, a quiz or a video.

TYPES OF FLY TRAP OFFERS™

| Guide | Template | Tool | Quiz | Video |

Give them a clear and compelling reason to give you their contact information. The best way: offer a simple resource that helps them solve a small problem.

Not a big problem (that's where your service comes in). Think of more of a "splinter" kind of problem. Something small, but painful/annoying, that you can quickly and easily solve for them. And make it easy for them to opt in.

OPTIN TOUCH POINTS

| Pop Up | Sticky Header | Inline Form | Link in Bio | Social DM |

Step 2: Get them to actually respond

This is where most businesses blow it.

They get a lead. Someone responds to their ad or fills out their contact form or requests a free consultation.

And they immediately pitch their services or try to book the appointment.

Instead, you need what I call The Yes/No Opener: a simple, casual, low-friction question designed to spark engagement.

You've already done all the hard work. You've advertised your business (external conversation) and tapped into the internal conversation in the mind of your market. Then you've given them a reason to raise their hand.

Don't waste the opportunity (like most service businesses do).

This is where you must insert your Proof of Life Protocol, a simple easy-to-answer question that is designed to do one thing: start a conversation.

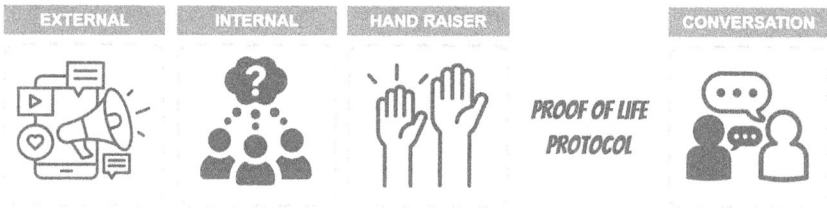

It must be a yes/no question. It must be easy to answer. And it must feel like the beginning of a conversation, not the start of a sales pitch.

Want to see my Proof of Life Protocol? Here it is:

Hey there! Gabriel here from GrowthMap. I can send you a demo here, yeah?

See how simple and conversational that is? The message is personalized, simple and clear. I want to make it easy for them to respond. Easy to start the conversation. Easy for me to help them.

Yours may be more formal.

Or maybe you keep it casual like me.

Regardless of your style, make it easy to answer.

What This Means for Your Business

Stop obsessing over lead quantity. Start obsessing over **conversation quality**.

Because remember... conversions happen in conversation.

And how much are those conversations worth?

If you could get just twice as many of your current leads to actually respond and engage, how much would that change your business?

My guess? It would change everything.

In the next chapter, we'll dive into Stage 3 of the Hook to Booked system: The Help. You'll learn exactly how to create prospects who convince themselves to buy before you ever make a pitch.

Because once you've got their attention and their engagement, it's time to build authority as THE go-to solution in their mind, which makes you the obvious choice.

CHAPTER 7

THE HELP:
Your Messaging Engine

How to Create Prospects Who Convince Themselves to Buy (Before You Ever Pitch)

Why 95% of Qualified Prospects Never Buy (And It's Not What You Think)

Here's what I see in almost every business I work with.

They've built a great system for attracting prospects.

They've built a great system for closing deals.

But they've completely ignored the middle of their funnel.

So prospects flow in, the ones who are ready to buy immediately convert, and everyone else leaks out, leaving all that money on the table.

It's like trying to fill a bucket with holes in it.

I call it Leaky Bucket Syndrome.

And it's the silent killer of sales.

It's the slow leak costing you profits. LOTS of profits.

But the solution isn't a bigger hose. It's fixing the holes.

And those holes get fixed with the right message delivered at the right time. Because the right message is exactly what your prospect needs to hear to make you the safe and obvious choice.

The Best Small Business Opportunity In The World

In 1954, Ray Kroc received an order for 8 of his Multimixers, a machine that could produce 5 milkshakes at the same time.

But nobody had ordered 8 Multimixers before, because nobody needed to be able to make that many milkshakes at once.

So Ray Kroc decided to personally fly out to San Bernardino, California. He wanted to see firsthand what kind of hamburger stand thought they needed 40 milkshakes being served at a time.

What he saw changed everything.

On the outside, he saw a hamburger stand run by 2 brothers and a small team of smiling teenagers.

But much like Neo seeing The Matrix for the first time, he instantly recognized something remarkable: a system that could produce consistent, quality food faster than anyone else in the industry.

Who were those two brothers?

Dick and Mac McDonald.

And from that initial meeting, Ray Kroc helped take the McDonald's brothers' single hamburger stand and turn it into "the best small-business opportunity in the world."

But here's what most people don't know about Ray Kroc's genius.

He didn't just copy their system.

He saw something the brothers missed entirely.

While the McDonald brothers were focused on running one really good restaurant, Kroc envisioned something bigger.

He realized he could package their system, their processes, their training methods, and their brand into something that could scale infinitely.

The brothers were working IN their business.

Kroc was working ON the business.

Within a decade, Ray Kroc had turned McDonald's into the largest restaurant chain in the world.

Not because he made better burgers.

But because he understood the power of leverage.

He created a turnkey model where each new restaurant owner received detailed operations manuals, training programs, and step-by-step procedures for everything from cooking fries to managing inventory.

He systematized the systematization.

The magic wasn't in the hamburgers. It was in the replicable, scalable system that made the hamburgers.

And that same principle applies to every service business today. The magic isn't in your talent or expertise alone. It's in building systems that can educate, nurture, and pre-qualify prospects automatically.

It's in the system that can take attention and turn it into **qualified** conversations.

The Archimedes Principle

Over 2,000 years ago, the Greek mathematician Archimedes made a profound observation about leverage.

"Give me a lever long enough and a fulcrum on which to place it, and I shall move the world."

He understood something that most people miss: the right system can amplify human effort exponentially.

The 5 Levers To Scale

Naval Ravikant, the legendary entrepreneur and investor behind AngelList, famously identified four types of leverage that separate successful entrepreneurs from everyone else.

As Naval puts it: "If you don't have leverage, you're never going to make real wealth. Leverage is the most important component of building a business."

But as I've worked with hundreds of service businesses, I've discovered a fifth lever that's becoming increasingly critical in our digital-first world.

Here are the 5 levers you can pull to get exponentially bigger results from less time and effort:

Naval's 4 Classic Levers:

Capital: Money working for you (investments, paid advertising, real estate)

Collaboration: People working for you (employees, agencies, partners)

Code: Technology working for you (automation, AI, custom apps)

Content: Media working for you (videos, emails, courses, frameworks)

The 5th Lever: Community

But there's one more lever that's rapidly emerging as the game-changer for service businesses.

As our world becomes increasingly digital (more AI, more automation, more robots) people will crave the opposite. They'll crave what's real, what's human, what's genuine.

Community: Networks working for you (referral systems, user groups, tribes of advocates, both online & in-person events)

The first two (**Capital** and **Collaboration**) still require additional investment as you scale.

More money to make more money.

More people to manage more people.

But the last three (**Code**, **Content**, and **Community**) have zero marginal cost.

They can scale infinitely without requiring proportional increases in time, money, or effort.

This is why the most successful service providers focus heavily on automation, content creation, and community building.

They're building systems that work 24/7/365, even when they're sleeping.

And here's what my smartest and richest friends & peers have discovered.

As our world becomes increasingly digital, community leverage becomes even more powerful. The businesses that can create genuine connection and belonging around their services will have an unfair advantage over those competing purely on features and price.

How Your Best Buyers' Brains Work (The Universal Truth About Human Psychology)

Our brains are biologically programmed to keep us safe.

Anything that feels potentially unsafe gets rejected automatically.

This served us well when we lived in tribes. When we slept in tents, susceptible to the elements, enemies and predators.

If we sensed something unsafe, our brains would alert us.

This kept us alive.

And not because it is logical.

But because it is neurological.

And it's exactly what happens when someone considers buying from you.

The moment they start thinking about making a purchase, their brain floods them with protective questions:

Can I trust this person?

What if this doesn't work?

What if I'm making a mistake?

Is this the right time?

Your job isn't to overcome these objections during a sales call.

Your job is to address them **before** the sales call ever happens.

Through stories. Through content. Through automated systems that build trust while you sleep.

That's how you make your service the safe solution in the mind of your market.

The Leverage Principle

I first learned this truth from Naval and it transformed how I think about business growth. Naval says:

"The most successful entrepreneurs are not the smartest or the hardest working. They are the best at using leverage."

This isn't about being lazy or looking for shortcuts.

It's about being strategic.

It's about building systems that can educate, nurture, and pre-qualify prospects automatically.

Systems that turn skeptical strangers into educated buyers who arrive at your sales conversations already convinced because they've been through your automations (Code) and they've read your emails & watched your videos (Content) and they've seen the proof & engagement you've generated online (Community).

Naval taught me about the 4 Levers to Scale.

When I applied them to my marketing and sales, everything changed.

When I taught them and helped my clients put the same levers into action in their businesses, the pattern became obvious.

There were only a few similarities I noticed among our most successful clients. The same 3 tools EVERY single one of them used in their marketing.

The Three-Prong Approach

Our most successful clients all use the same three-prong approach when it comes to following up with leads.

After someone raises their hand and becomes a lead, but before you have the opportunity to have a sales conversation and pitch your services, you've got to educate your clients.

Because educated clients are the best clients.

And these are the 3 tools every top producer and successful entrepreneur uses to follow up, nurture and educate new leads:

Automation: Workflows that send emails, text messages and videos to new leads without any human intervention (Code + Content)

AI: AI Agents that can follow up with new leads, answer basic questions and book appointments without sounding like a bot (Code)

Personal Outreach: Strategic personal touch at high-impact moments (Collaboration)

They use Code and Content (AI + Automation) to do the heavy lifting.

Then they use Collaboration (Personal Outreach) strategically, only where human touch & manual effort provides the highest return.

Just like what Ray Kroc saw in the McDonald's brothers' system, the biggest winners are those that use technology and media to get more done in less time, and they use personal touch to build trust and connection with their clients.

This allows them to engage with 10 times more prospects than their competitors while working fewer hours.

That's leverage.

What This Means for Your Business

Stop trying to manually follow up with every prospect.

Start building a system that does the nurturing for you.

Create content that addresses the most common objections before prospects even think to ask them. Use automation to deliver the right message at the right time to the right person. And save your personal energy for the conversations that matter most.

In the next chapter, we'll dive into Stage 4 of the Hook to Booked system: The Handoff.

You'll learn exactly how to transition educated, pre-qualified prospects into booked appointments that actually show up.

Because all the leverage in the world won't help you if you can't convert engaged prospects into paying clients.

CHAPTER 8

THE HANDOFF:
The Triple-Lock System That Guarantees Qualified Appointments

How to Book Them, Keep Them, and Prime Them to Buy Before You Ever Meet

The 73% Problem That's Killing Your Calendar

What if I told you that nearly 3 out of 4 sales appointments are completely worthless?

Not because the prospects aren't qualified.

Not because they don't need what you're selling.

But because they show up unprepared, uninformed, and unconvinced that you're the right choice.

Studies show that only about 27% of leads are ready to make a buying decision when they first reach out to a service provider.

That means 73% of the appointments on your calendar are prospects who need education, trust-building, and objection handling before they can buy.

No wonder sales feel so hard.

You're making your sales appointments do all the heavy lifting.

But what if we flipped it?

What if every single appointment on your calendar showed up already convinced you're the right choice?

What if they arrived educated, pre-qualified, and ready to buy?

The $1.7 Million Presentation Mistake

In 1985, Steve Jobs made one of the most expensive presentation mistakes in business history.

He was pitching the revolutionary Macintosh computer to a room full of skeptical business executives. The stakes couldn't have been higher. Apple needed corporate sales to survive.

Jobs walked into that boardroom confident that his brilliant product would sell itself. He had the best technology, the most innovative features, and a computer that would change everything.

But he made one critical error.

He assumed that because his audience had agreed to the meeting, they were ready to buy.

He was wrong.

The executives sat stone-faced as Jobs demonstrated the Mac's capabilities. They asked technical questions he couldn't answer. They raised concerns about compatibility he hadn't addressed.

They walked away unconvinced, and Apple lost millions in potential enterprise sales.

The lesson? Even the most revolutionary product fails when the audience isn't properly prepared.

Jobs learned this lesson well, which is why his later presentations became legendary for their careful audience preparation and education.

The Coffee Shop Revelation

Sometimes the best ideas show up in the most unexpected places.

I was having coffee with my friend Mike, catching up on life and family when the conversation naturally drifted to business.

Mike had left his corporate CEO job in 2020 to start his own consulting practice. He wasn't a marketer by trade, just a founder with the heart of a teacher who genuinely cared about every person in his orbit.

What he shared next immediately caught my attention.

Mike sells to credit union CEOs. Not an easy crowd to impress.

"As soon as someone books on my calendar," Mike told me, "I pull out my phone and record a short video. 30 to 45 seconds tops."

"What do you say?" I asked.

"I just tell them I'm excited to meet with them. I share three specific questions I'm going to ask on our call, so they know what we'll discuss. That's really it."

"Just a short personal intro. Then I text them that video immediately."

Here's the part that blew me away.

"Gabriel, I get a response 100% of the time. Every single person replies to that text. They appreciate it, it stands out, and it really sets us up for success."

That's when it hit me.

Mike had stumbled upon something most service providers completely miss: the power of personal connection in the moments after booking.

He wasn't just confirming appointments. **He was priming prospects for success.**

The Two Conversations at Booking

Remember what we learned about the two conversations happening in every interaction? The external and internal convos?

When someone books an appointment with you, there are two conversations that kick off right away:

External Conversation (You): You send a confirmation email & text message. "Thanks for booking. Here's your confirmation... here's what we'll cover... here's how we can help you..."

Internal Conversation (Them): Their mind starts racing. "Did I make the right choice? What if this is a waste of time? What if they try to pressure me? Should I cancel? Maybe I should keep looking for other options..."

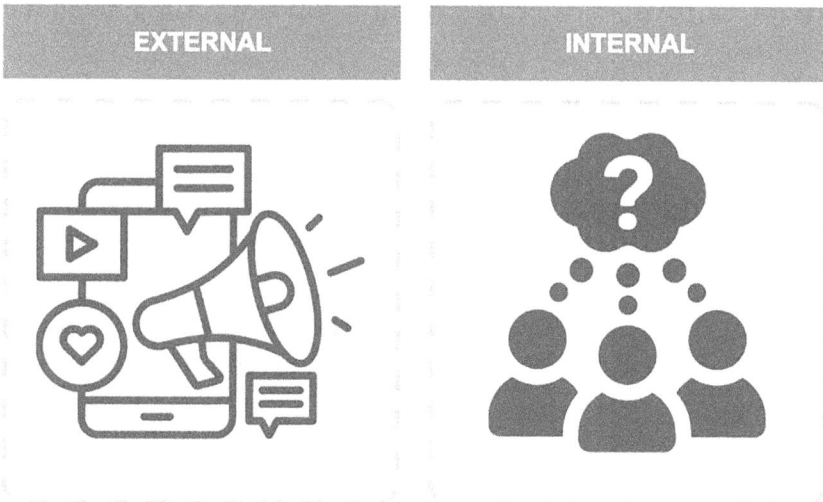

That internal conversation is working against you every moment between booking and meeting.

But when you reach out immediately with a personal touch, like Mike's video messages, something magical happens:

External Conversation: "Wow, they sent me a personal video."

Internal Conversation: "These people actually care. They're professional. This feels different. I made the right choice."

The handoff transforms doubt into confidence before you ever meet.

But what needs to happen before the appointment to make closing effortless?

The 4 Closes Framework

Before a prospect decides to buy, you don't have to make one sale.

You actually have to make four.

Because there are only 4 reasons a prospect doesn't buy. And no, price is not one of those reasons.

So if we know the 4 reasons why they won't buy, we know exactly what we need to close them on so buying becomes automatic.

Close #1: Trust You

They must believe you're competent and credible (you and your company)

Close #2: Trust the Path

They must believe your process and approach will work

Close #3: Trust Your Product

They must believe your specific offer is right for them

Close #4: Trust Themselves

They must believe they can succeed with your help

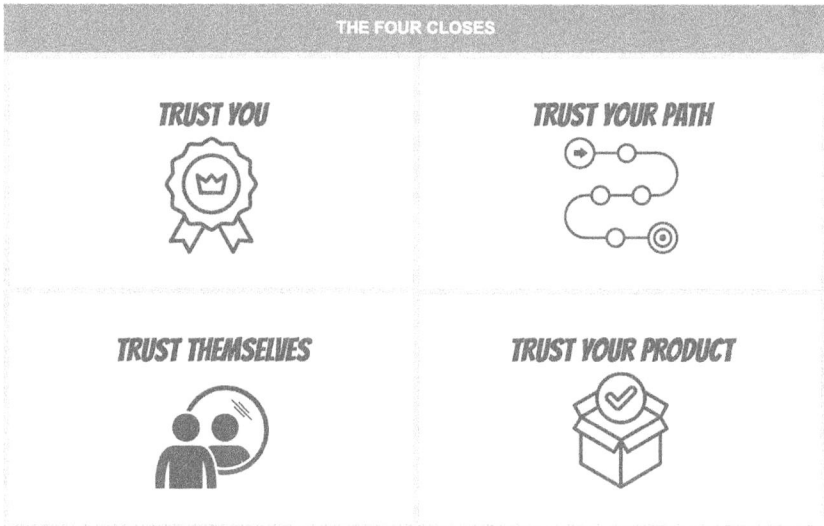

THE FOUR CLOSES

TRUST YOU

TRUST YOUR PATH

TRUST THEMSELVES

TRUST YOUR PRODUCT

Most service providers wait until the sales call to address these four closes.

But by then, it's too late. The prospect's mind is already made up. They're either convinced or they're not.

But if you can start addressing The 4 Closes **before** your sales conversation, your close rate will skyrocket.

The Educational Advantage

Here's the principle that will transform your sales process:

"The best buyers are educated buyers."

Statistics show that prospects who consume 20-40 minutes of your content before a sales conversation close at dramatically higher rates.

But it can't just be any content.

It must be strategic content that speaks to the four closes:

- Stories that build trust in you and your expertise
- Case studies that demonstrate your path works
- Testimonials that showcase your product in action
- Success stories that help them trust themselves to succeed

Once your prospect consumes this kind of content, they've already answered their own objections. They've already convinced themselves you understand their problem. They've already seen evidence that your approach works.

They're not coming to be sold. They're coming to buy.

The Triple-Lock Implementation

Here's the blueprint for booking more meetings and making the most of every appointment on your calendar:

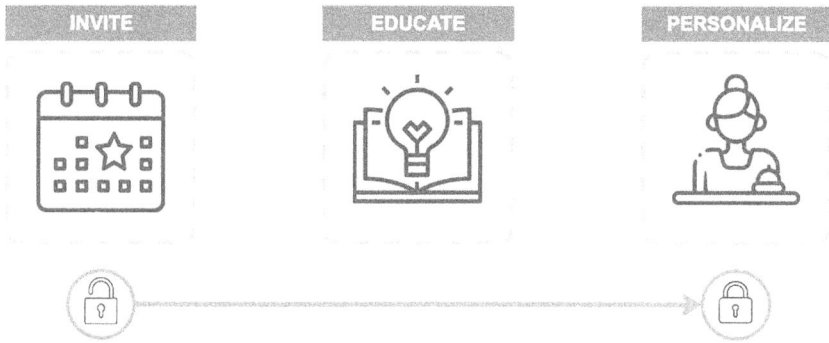

Lock #1: Make the invitation

Ask permission to help them solve their problem with a soft, consultative approach

Lock #2: Educate to build trust

Send content (via automated workflows & AI) that addresses all four closes between booking and meeting

Lock #3: Personalize to connect

Add a human touch with personalized video messages that build connection

Our most successful clients combine automation with personalization. They use systems to deliver consistent education, then add personal audio & video messages that make prospects feel seen and understood.

Like Mike's simple 30-second video that gets a 100% response rate.

What This Means for Your Business

Stop putting so much pressure on your sales calls.

Start priming the pump earlier in the process.

The time between "yes, I'll meet with you" and the actual meeting is when the real selling happens.

Use that time to educate, build trust, and address objections through stories and content.

By the time they sit down with you, they should already be convinced you're the right choice.

Because if you've gotten them to this point, you've done the hard part:

- You've captured their attention with a solid **Hook**
- You've taken them off the market and **Held** their attention
- You've proven that you can **Help** so they're open to your offer
- And you've earned the right to make the **Handoff** and close the sale

But it's one thing to know **what to do** to grow your business.

It's another thing entirely to know **how to do it**.

Which is exactly what we'll cover in the final section and the last few chapters of this book.

You'll discover exactly how to implement these strategies at scale so you can focus on serving clients instead of chasing prospects.

Because the goal isn't just to book more appointments.

It's to build a system that builds your business.

PART III

BUILDING YOUR SYSTEM

From Framework to Wealth Machine

The GrowthMap Model™

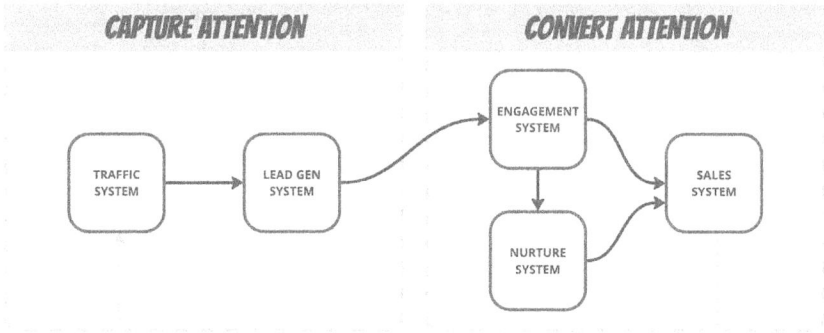

CAPTURE ATTENTION   CONVERT ATTENTION

TRAFFIC SYSTEM → LEAD GEN SYSTEM → ENGAGEMENT SYSTEM → NURTURE SYSTEM → SALES SYSTEM

Strangers → Lurkers → Leads → Conversations → Clients → Cash

CHAPTER 9

YOUR WEALTH MACHINE:
The System That Works While You Sleep

How to Turn Everything You've Learned Into a Predictable Client Acquisition Engine

The Choice Every Service Business Owner Must Make

Right now, you're standing at the same crossroads where I found myself in that Build-A-Bear parking lot.

You have two paths in front of you:

Path 1: Close this book, hope things get better on their own, and keep doing what you've always done.

Path 2: Take what you've learned and build the system that transforms your business forever.

Most business owners choose Path 1.

They read, they learn, they get excited. But they never implement.

Or they start something that could actually give them what they want. But never see it all the way through.

They stay trapped in the feast-or-famine cycle, chasing leads instead of attracting them, working IN their business instead of ON it.

But you're not most business owners.

You wouldn't have read this far if you were satisfied with mediocre results.

The Two Conversations at Decision Time

As you consider what to do next, notice the two conversations happening in your mind right now:

External Conversation: "This all makes sense. I should implement these strategies."

Internal Conversation: "But where do I start? What if I mess it up? What if I don't have time? What if it doesn't work for my business? Maybe I should just try to figure this out myself..."

Sound familiar?

This is exactly what your prospects experience when they consider buying from you.

The difference between successful entrepreneurs and everyone else isn't that they don't have these internal conversations.

It's that they take action despite them.

We tell our kids all the time…

Being brave isn't about getting rid of fear.

It's about doing the thing, even when you're afraid.

The Constraint That's Choking Your Growth

Let me ask you a direct question:

What's the biggest constraint in your business right now?

Most service business owners immediately say "I need more leads."

But is that really true?

What if you don't need more leads?

What if you just need more qualified conversations?

The real constraints are usually:

- **Speed-to-Lead:** You're losing most opportunities because you respond too slowly
- **Follow-Up Systems:** You have no systematic way to nurture prospects who aren't ready to buy immediately
- **Authority Positioning:** Your prospects don't see you as the obvious choice in your market
- **Conversion Process:** You're making sales calls do all the heavy lifting instead of pre-qualifying prospects

Here's the truth: **Your business is exactly one system away from breakthrough.**

The Wealth Machine Blueprint

Everything you've learned in this book points to one inevitable conclusion:

You need to build what I call your **Wealth Machine**.

A systematic approach to client acquisition that:

1. **Captures attention** from the people you are uniquely meant to serve
2. **Converts attention into leads** and gets people to raise their hand
3. **Builds authority and trust** through strategic content and follow-up
4. **Transitions prospects into sales conversations** where they're already convinced you're the right choice

This isn't just marketing theory. This is how reality works.

The GrowthMap Model™

After building multiple seven-figure businesses and working with 300+ service professionals, I've discovered the pattern that every successful business follows.

It's the same thing Ray Kroc saw in the McDonald's brothers' system — a predictable, repeatable process. But instead of turning raw ingredients into hamburgers, your Wealth Machine turns strangers into eager, ready-to-buy clients.

Just like the human body is made up of smaller systems working together, your client acquisition system consists of five integrated systems:

The GrowthMap Model™

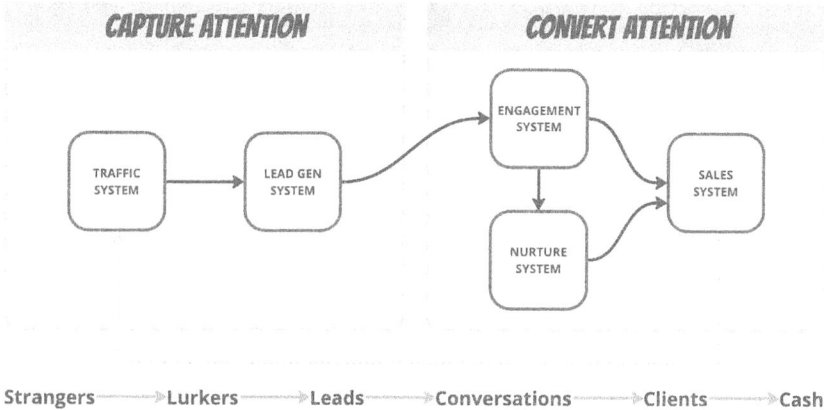

CAPTURE ATTENTION	CONVERT ATTENTION

```
                              ┌──────────────┐
                              │  ENGAGEMENT  │
                              │    SYSTEM    │
                              └──────┬───────┘
 ┌─────────┐     ┌─────────┐         │         ┌─────────┐
 │ TRAFFIC │────▶│ LEAD GEN│─────┐   ▼     ┌──▶│  SALES  │
 │ SYSTEM  │     │ SYSTEM  │     │         │   │ SYSTEM  │
 └─────────┘     └─────────┘     └──┐  ┌───┘   └─────────┘
                              ┌─────▼──┴─────┐
                              │   NURTURE    │
                              │   SYSTEM     │
                              └──────────────┘
```

Strangers----▶Lurkers----▶Leads----▶Conversations----▶Clients----▶Cash

System 1: Traffic System (Capture Attention)

How you increase reach and visibility, attracting ideal customers

- Content that stops the scroll and speaks to internal conversations
- Consistent presence where your prospects already hang out
- Authority positioning that makes you the obvious choice

System 2: Lead Gen System (Capture Attention)

How you convert attention into hand-raisers

- Fly Trap Offers™ that turn lurkers into leads
- Compelling reasons for prospects to raise their hand

- Clear value propositions that resonate with your market

System 3: Engagement System (Convert Attention)

How you get new leads into conversation and take them off the market

- Speed-to-lead response that captures prospects at their tipping point
- AI and automation that qualifies prospects 24/7/365
- Personal touch that creates human connection at scale

System 4: Nurture System (Convert Attention)

How you stay top-of-mind until prospects are ready to buy

- Educational content that addresses the 4 Closes before sales conversations
- Automated sequences that build trust while you sleep
- Belief-shifting content that keeps you positioned as the authority

System 5: Sales System (Convert Attention)

How you enroll qualified prospects into your services

- Triple-Lock appointment process that ensures qualified meetings
- Educational bridge that primes prospects to buy before they meet you
- Conversion framework that makes closing feel natural and consultative

The Implementation Reality

Here's what happens when most people try to implement these strategies on their own:

Week 1: High motivation. They start working on their Hook strategy.

Week 2: Still excited. They begin creating their Fly Trap Offer™.

Week 3: Momentum slows. Other priorities demand attention.

Week 4: Implementation stalls. They get overwhelmed by all the moving pieces. Or distracted by some shiny object. Or both.

Week 8: They're back to their old patterns, wondering why "nothing works."

Sound familiar?

The problem isn't the strategy. The strategy works.

The problem is trying to build a sophisticated system while also running a business.

The Two Conversations About Getting Help

Right now, you're probably having another internal conversation:

External Conversation: "I could probably figure this out myself."

Internal Conversation: "But when would I find the time? What if I build it wrong? What if I waste months going down the wrong path? What if I could get help from someone who's already done this successfully?"

Here's what I've learned after building systems for hundreds of businesses:

The entrepreneurs who try to figure it out alone usually take 2-3 years to get results (if they get results at all).

The entrepreneurs who get systematic guidance from someone who's already built this successfully usually see results in 60-90 days.

Which path makes more sense for your business?

Which path gets you to your $100k months faster?

What This Means for Your Business

You have everything you need to transform your business.

You understand why people buy (when pain peaks from whoever is top-of-mind and trusted).

You know how to speak to both conversations (external and internal).

You've learned the importance of speed (money loves speed).

You understand the four-stage system that turns strangers into buyers.

But knowledge without implementation is just expensive entertainment.

The System That Builds Systems

The most successful service business owners don't just build great businesses.

They build systems that build great businesses.

They create a **Wealth Machine** that generates consistent, qualified conversations and eager ready-to-buy clients automatically.

They buy back their time with automation and AI.

They scale without sacrificing their personal life or burning out their team.

They work 4 days a week while adding an extra $100k+ per month to their business. They continually level up and systematically increase sales every year.

This isn't fantasy. This is how the top 1% of service providers actually operate.

Your Next Decision Point

You're at another Build-A-Bear moment.

You can put this book down and hope things get better on their own.

Or you can take the next step and build the Wealth Machine that transforms your business forever.

The choice is yours.

But remember: **Every day you delay is another day your competitors are capturing the prospects who should be buying from you.**

Every day you don't have a systematic approach to client acquisition is another day you're leaving money on the table.

Every day you work IN your business instead of ON it is another day you're trading time for money instead of building wealth.

The Path Forward

In the next chapter, I'll show you exactly how to implement your Wealth Machine using the same process that's helped hundreds of service businesses break through their revenue ceiling.

You'll learn the step-by-step roadmap that takes you from where you are now to consistent $100k+ months.

Because you've invested the time to learn these strategies.

Now it's time to put them to work.

Your Wealth Machine is waiting to be built.

The only question is: **When do you want to start?**

CHAPTER 10

THE ROADMAP:
From Framework to
Wealth Machine

Your Step-by-Step Plan to Build the System
That Adds $100k+ Month to Your Business

The Truth About Implementation

You now understand the Hook to Booked Blueprint™.

You know the principles that separate thriving businesses from struggling ones.

You've learned the GrowthMap Model™ that puts Hook to Booked Blueprint™ into action and turns strangers into eager buyers.

But there's a critical difference between knowing what to do and actually doing it systematically.

The businesses that break through to $100k+ months only working 3-4 days a week don't just understand the framework — they follow a proven implementation process.

They're the ones that take systematic action on what they've learned.

The $100K Implementation Challenge

Most entrepreneurs approach implementation backwards.

They try to build everything at once, get overwhelmed, and end up building nothing.

But successful business owners follow a different path. They understand that **constraint elimination beats random optimization every time.**

Instead of trying to fix everything, they identify their biggest bottleneck and eliminate it first.

Then they find the next constraint and eliminate that one.

This systematic approach is exactly how we've helped hundreds of service businesses break through their revenue ceiling to consistent $100k+ months.

The Clarity Compass™: Your Diagnostic Tool

Before you can fix your business, you need to know what's actually broken.

Most entrepreneurs guess at their constraints. Professionals diagnose them.

The Clarity Compass™ is the diagnostic tool I use with every client to identify exactly which part of their Wealth Machine needs attention first.

Here's how it works:

Step 1: The Five-System Assessment

Grade each system in your Wealth Machine on a scale of Red, Yellow, or Green:

Traffic System (Capture Attention)

- Red: No consistent way to generate visibility
- Yellow: Some traffic but inconsistent or limited reach
- Green: Predictable, scalable attention from multiple sources

Lead Generation System (Capture Attention)

- Red: Only way to become a lead is to book a sales call
- Yellow: Have some lead magnets but low conversion rates
- Green: Multiple compelling reasons for prospects to raise their hand

Engagement System (Convert Attention)

- Red: Taking hours or days to respond to new leads
- Yellow: Usually respond quickly but no systematic follow-up
- Green: Consistent speed-to-lead and high response rate from new leads

Nurture System (Convert Attention)

- Red: No systematic way to stay in touch with prospects
- Yellow: Send occasional emails but no strategic sequence
- Green: Automated system that builds trust and addresses objections

Sales System (Convert Attention)

- Red: Winging it on sales calls with inconsistent results
- Yellow: Have a process but appointments feel like starting from scratch
- Green: Prospects arrive educated and ready to buy

Step 2: Identify Your Top 1-2 Constraints

Circle the systems that are Red or Yellow. These are your constraints.

Now prioritize them based on impact. Which constraint, if eliminated, would make the biggest difference to your revenue in the next 90 days?

That's where you start.

Green: Strengths that you can leave alone (for now)

Yellow: Areas you could improve

Red: Your biggest opportunities for growth

CAPTURE ATTENTION		CONVERT ATTENTION	
TRAFFIC SYSTEM		**ENGAGEMENT SYSTEM**	
	Attention Generating Assets / CONTENT / Attention Converting Assets	**NURTURE SYSTEM**	
LEAD GEN SYSTEM		**SALES SYSTEM**	

Strangers ····▷ Lurkers ····▷ Leads ····▷ Conversations ····▷ Clients ····▷ Cash

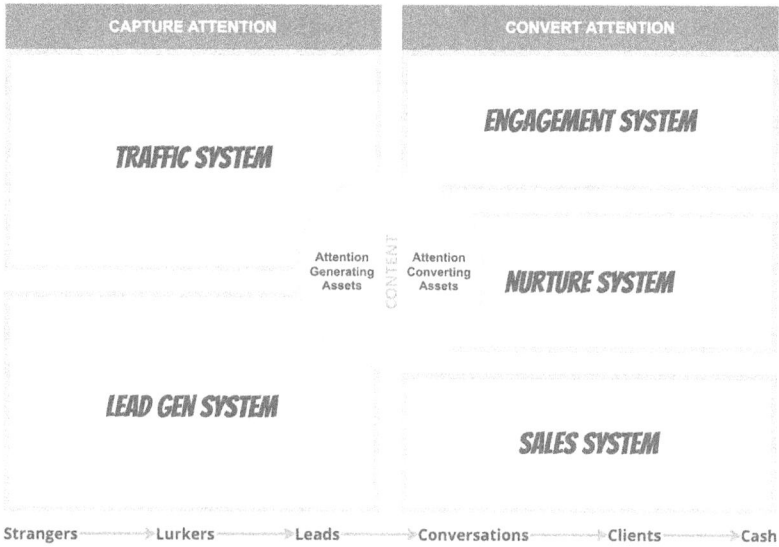

The Three-Phase Implementation Path

Based on working with 300+ service businesses, I've identified the three phases every successful Wealth Machine follows:

Phase 1: Foundation (30 Days)

Goal: Stop the bleeding, create immediate wins and map your system

Priority Constraints:

- Speed-to-lead response (if Red)
- Basic lead generation system (if Red)
- Minimum viable sales process (if Red)

Outcome: Consistent lead flow and improved conversion of existing traffic

Phase 2: Systemization + Acceleration (90 Days)

Goal: Build the system (fill the gaps) and scale what's working

Priority Constraints:

- Traffic generation and authority building
- Systematic nurture sequences
- Advanced lead qualification

Outcome: Predictable pipeline of qualified prospects

Phase 3: Optimization (12+ Months)

Goal: Maximize conversations & sales and build the empire

Priority Constraints:

- Multi-channel traffic strategies
- Advanced automation and AI
- Referral and expansion systems

Outcome: $100k+ months with predictable growth in 3-4 days / week

The System Architecture Decision

Here's where most business owners get stuck. They know what to build, but they don't know how to build it.

You have three options:

Option 1: Build It Yourself

Pros: Complete control, potentially lower upfront cost **Cons:** 2-3 years to see results, high failure rate, opportunity cost **Best For:** Entrepreneurs who have unlimited time and love learning marketing technology

Option 2: Hire an Agency

Pros: Professional execution, don't have to learn the tech **Cons:** Expensive ($10-20k/month), still need to manage the relationship, often focused on tactics not systems **Best For:** Businesses already doing $5M+ annually with dedicated marketing budgets

Option 3: Get Systematic Guidance

Pros: Learn while you build, faster results, comprehensive approach **Cons:** Requires investment in systems, coaching & training **Best For:** Service businesses ready to invest in building their Wealth Machine the right way

The Professional Advantage

Here's what I've learned after building multiple seven-figure businesses:

The entrepreneurs who get systematic guidance don't just get better results faster. They get exponentially better results.

Why? Because they avoid the three implementation killers that destroy most DIY attempts:

Implementation Killer #1: Shiny Object Syndrome

The Problem: Getting distracted by new tactics before completing the system

The Solution: Having a clear roadmap and someone to keep you on track

Implementation Killer #2: Technical Overwhelm

The Problem: Getting stuck on technology instead of focusing on strategy

The Solution: Proven templates, step-by-step processes and concierge support

Implementation Killer #3: Isolation Paralysis

The Problem: Having no one to turn to when you get stuck

The Solution: Expert guidance and peer community (rising tide lifts all boats)

The Compound Effect of Systems

When you build your Wealth Machine the right way, something magical happens. It's not just that you get more leads or close more sales.

It's that every part of your business starts working better together.

Your Traffic System feeds your Lead Gen System.

Your Lead Gen System feeds your Engagement System.

Your Engagement System feeds your Nurture System.

Your Nurture System feeds your Sales System.

And your Sales System creates happy clients who become your best source of new traffic.

This is what I call the Freedom Flywheel™. Once it's spinning, it becomes easier to maintain than to stop.

The Implementation Reality Check

Building a Wealth Machine isn't a weekend project.

It requires focus, consistency, and the right guidance.

But here's what our most successful clients have in common:

They don't try to figure it out alone.

They understand that time is their most valuable asset. They'd rather invest in proven guidance than waste months (or years) trying to figure it out themselves.

They follow a systematic process that's been tested with hundreds of businesses. They adopt a "who not how" approach.

They find the "who" that has the "how" to move faster (money loves speed).

They focus on one constraint at a time instead of trying to fix everything at once.

Your Next Decision

You're standing at the same crossroads where every successful entrepreneur has stood.

You can try to figure this out yourself and hope for the best.

Or you can get the systematic guidance that compresses your learning curve from years to months.

The entrepreneurs who choose the guidance path don't just get their Wealth Machine built faster.

They get it built right.

They avoid the costly mistakes that derail most DIY attempts.

They have someone to turn to when they get stuck.

Most importantly, they focus on serving clients instead of figuring out marketing technology.

What This Means for Your Business

Your Wealth Machine is waiting to be built.

You have the framework. You understand the principles. You know what needs to be done.

The only question is: **How quickly do you want to get there?**

Every day you delay building your systematic approach to client acquisition is another day your competitors are capturing prospects who should be buying from you.

Every day you work harder instead of smarter is another day you're trading time for money instead of building wealth.

In the conclusion, I'll share the most important decision you'll make for your business this year.

Because everything you've learned in this book comes down to one simple choice.

A choice that will determine whether you're still struggling with feast-or-famine a year from now...

Or whether you're enjoying the freedom and predictability of $100k+ months while working just three or four days a week.

The choice is yours.

But first, you need to understand why most people never make this choice at all.

CONCLUSION
Where Do We Go From Here

Congratulations!

You've just completed a journey that most business owners never take.

You've learned the principles that separate thriving service businesses from struggling ones.

You understand the Hook to Booked Blueprint™ that turns strangers into eager buyers.

You know the GrowthMap Model™ that creates predictable $100k+ months.

Most importantly, you've discovered that **you don't need more leads — you need more qualified conversations.**

This isn't just a marketing insight. It's a fundamental law that governs every successful service business.

And now you have the framework to make it work for you.

Your Path Forward

If you want to stop chasing prospects and start having qualified clients chase you, then consider joining my next Hook to Booked Workshop.

With it, you'll get the complete implementation blueprint, proven templates, and step-by-step guidance that will help you build your automated client acquisition system in less than 30 days.

And the best part? You'll leave with everything you need to implement immediately.

No more guessing. No more overwhelm. Just a clear path to predictable growth.

Ready to **automate where attention flows** so you can **systematize where sales go**?

Reserve your seat at: **HookToBooked.com/workshop**

The Most Important Decision

Picture yourself three years from now.

Where do you want to be? Maybe it's working only three or four days a week while your business runs itself. Maybe it's having the freedom to take that family vacation without checking your phone every five minutes.

Whatever your goal is, hold that picture in your mind.

Now here's the reality: Three years will pass whether you take action today or not. Time doesn't care about your intentions. It only responds to your decisions.

Your Four Futures

And there are exactly four futures waiting for you:

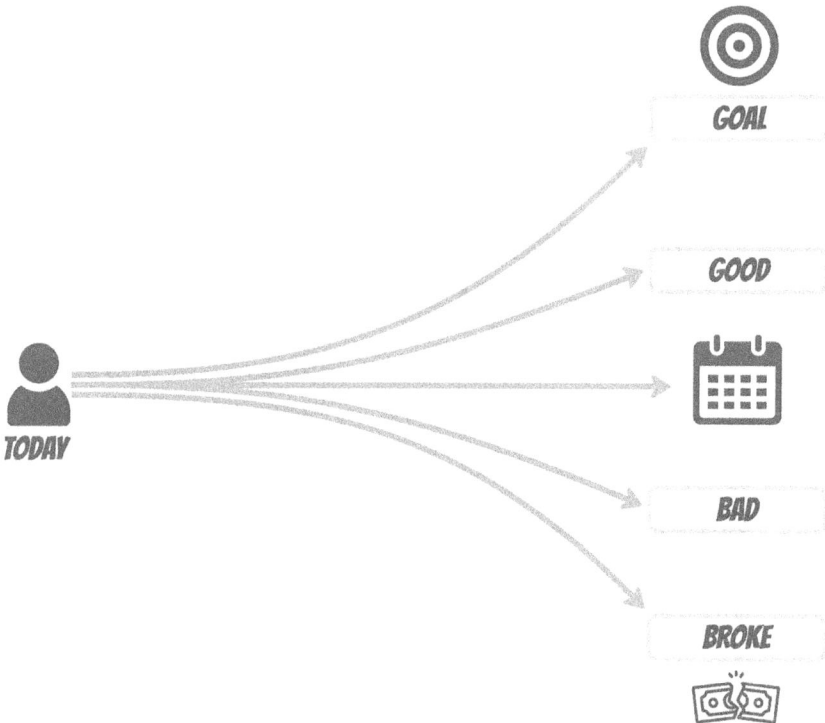

Future #1: You Hit Your Target — Everything clicks. Your Wealth Machine is humming. Qualified clients are reaching out to you instead of you chasing prospects. You've got more time & freedom. This is the bullseye.

Future #2: You Land in "Good Enough" — You make some improvements. Business is a little better than today, but nowhere near your potential. You're still overworked, still underpaid, left wondering what could have been.

Future #3: You Actually Go Backwards — Market conditions change. Competitors get smarter. Tech and marketing keeps changing faster. You get left behind. Three years later, somehow in a worse position than you are today.

Future #4: You End Up Broke — You keep doing what you've always done. The feast-or-famine cycle eventually breaks you. You're forced to close the business. The dream dies.

Here's what most entrepreneurs don't realize: **Today, you're closest to the line that leads to "good enough."**

Every day you delay building the right system, every week you put off taking decisive action, you drift further from the bullseye and closer to mediocrity.

The entrepreneurs who hit their targets don't wait for perfect conditions. They don't spend months researching every option. They recognize the moment of decision and they act.

They understand that the gap between where they are and where they want to be isn't about time.

It's about systems.

So which future are you choosing?

Because make no mistake: Not choosing IS choosing.

If you want to hit the bullseye instead of settling for "good enough," the time to build your Wealth Machine is now.

Not next month when things slow down. Not next quarter when you have more time. Now.

While you still have momentum from everything you've learned in this book.

Three years will pass.

The only question is: Which future will you be living?

But before you make any decision about the workshop, I want to share a story that changed my life forever.

Because what I learned in that moment will determine whether you transform your business this year or stay stuck in the same patterns that have been holding you back.

The Conversation That Changes Everything

Remember at the beginning of this book when I shared about moving my family from Bend, Oregon to Las Vegas, Nevada, back to Bend, Oregon, and finally to Nashville, Tennessee?

All in less than 90 days.

There's a lesson I learned through that experience that I'm forever grateful for, but hope I never have to go through something like that again to learn.

Sitting in that Build-A-Bear parking lot on my daughter's sixth birthday, I was faced with a decision.

I could keep doing what I was already doing, even though I didn't like the results I was getting.

Or I could make a change.

It's tempting to do nothing. To stay comfortable. To convince yourself that things will somehow magically improve if you keep doing the same thing.

But here's what I've learned: **the people who take decisive action when they know something needs to change are the ones who deserve the rewards that follow.**

In that moment, sitting in the parking lot with my family inside celebrating, I made the decision to get help.

I called my friend Matt for perspective. I reached out to my coach — a guy with gray hair, wisdom, and the kind of life I hoped to build.

But I didn't just take ideas and talk about what I could do.

I got into motion. I took decisive action.

That day. Not the next day. Not a week later. That day.

I walked into Build-A-Bear and told my wife my decision. We spent the afternoon celebrating our daughter's birthday. Then that night, I packed our entire house, loaded up the truck and U-Haul, and hit the road.

Fast forward four years later, and it was the best decision I'd ever made.

When I ask our kids about their favorite place to live... Southern California, Central Oregon, or Tennessee... they resoundingly say Tennessee. They talk about their friends, the community, their school, the life they have here.

None of which they would have if I hadn't taken action.

Your Build-A-Bear Moment

Right now, you're sitting in your own Build-A-Bear parking lot.

You know what you need to do. You have the framework. You understand the principles.

The only question is: **Will you take action?**

As entrepreneurs, we're so tied to our businesses that it's often difficult to distinguish between ourselves and what we've built. But you only get one life, so you might as well make it count.

Obviously, I would love to connect and help you build the business you've always dreamed of. But if now's not the right time, that's okay too.

All I ask is this: **Do something.**

Take some sort of action, some sort of step forward.

Ask yourself: *What's worth the next 10 years of my life?*

Because once you find that answer, life gets a whole lot better.

The Choice Is Yours

You can close this book and hope things get better on their own.

Or you can take the next step and build the business you've always dreamed of.

The entrepreneurs who choose action don't just get better results.

They get the life they actually want.

They work when they want while their competitors work nonstop.

They have predictable growth while others struggle with feast-or-famine.

They build wealth instead of just trading time for money.

Most importantly, they get their time back to spend with the people they love most.

Remember: **99% of service businesses are one system away from breakthrough.**

The question isn't whether this system works. The question is whether you'll build it.

Your Next Step

Ready to transform your business and your life?

Reserve your seat at **HookToBooked.com/workshop** and take the first step toward the business you've always dreamed of.

Even if you decide the workshop isn't for you, please do something with what you've learned.

Your future self will thank you for taking action today.

Let's build your system.

~ Gabriel Ryan

P.S. If something isn't worth the next 10 years of your life, it's not worth 10 minutes of your attention. But if you've read this far, I think you know what's worth your next 10 years. The only question is: when do you want to start?

ABOUT THE AUTHOR

Gabriel Ryan is an entrepreneur and growth strategist. After a decade as a professional photographer, he helped scale a digital marketing agency in the Financial Publishing industry to $25M annually and later launched a software company that hit $140K monthly recurring revenue in under nine months.

Following a pivotal moment in a Build-A-Bear parking lot, Gabriel founded GrowthMap, where he has helped 300+ service businesses design and deploy client acquisition systems. His Hook-to-Booked Blueprint™ helps service providers turn strangers into ready-to-buy clients, generating millions in revenue worldwide.

Gabriel lives in Nashville, Tennessee with his wife Carlie and their four children. His mission is simple: to help entrepreneurs build businesses that buy back time and create freedom.

Scan the QR code to connect with Gabriel on Instagram @gabrielryan and access free resources, strategies, and behind-the-scenes insights.

www.ingramcontent.com/pod-product-compliance
Lightning Source LLC
Chambersburg PA
CBHW061255220326
41599CB00028B/5657